KnitLit
(TOO)

ALSO EDITED BY LINDA ROGHAAR AND MOLLY WOLF

KnitLit: Sweaters and Their Stories . . .
and Other Writing About Knitting

LINDA ROGHAAR *&* MOLLY WOLF, EDITORS

KnitLit
(TOO)

Stories from Sheep to Shawl...
And More Writing About Knitting

THREE RIVERS PRESS • NEW YORK

"Temporarily Almost a Blanket" by Terry Miller Shannon first appeared in a slightly different form in *The Christian Science Monitor*. "I'm Gonna Sit Right Down and Knit Myself a Sweater" lyrics © 2003 by Jody Kolodzey; originally published in the Spring 2003 issue of *Sing Out!* magazine (Vol. 47, No. 1), page 88. "Real Men Knit" by Dawn Goldsmith first appeared in a slightly different form in *The Christian Science Monitor*. "Dropped Stitches" by Helen Kay Polaski was first published in *Bonzer!* "Sweaters" copyright © 2004 by Lesléa Newman. "The Whole World in My Hands" by Dayna Macy originally appeared in a slightly different version on Salon.com. "Mariah Educates the Sensitive" by Susan Blackwell Ramsey from *Rhino 2002*; reprinted with the permission of the author.

Published by Three Rivers Press, New York, New York.
Member of the Crown Publishing Group, a division of Random House, Inc.
www.crownpublishing.com

THREE RIVERS PRESS and the Tugboat design are registered trademarks of Random House, Inc.

Printed in the United States of America

Design by Joy O'Meara-Battista

Library of Congress Cataloging-in-Publication Data
Knitlit too: stories from sheep to shawl—and more writing about knitting / Linda Roghaar and Molly Wolf, Editors.
[1. Knitting.] I. Roghaar, Linda. II. Wolf, Molly.
TT820 .K6945 2004
746.43'2—dc22   2003018422

ISBN 1-4000-5149-5

10 9 8 7 6 5 4 3

First Edition

For Florence Bigelow Roghaar

*And for our blokes, Jay and Henry, with love. C'mere, guys;
we'll put down our knitting and give you a hug.*

ABOUT THE COVER: *Still Life*, by Margaret Klein Wilson

Looking at a basket of my yarn, I wonder, "What next?" A bouquet of freshly dyed skeins is both a summation and a starting point, the expectant pause between two creative processes. First, a year of anticipation as sheep move through their seasons between shearings: lambing, grazing good grass, starry nights, and snowy days. An armful of newly shorn fleece is warm, lively, and telling, mute homage to a thousand happy collaborations between sheep, shepherd, and the natural world. Spun into yarn and dyed, the fleece is transformed. It is energy briefly at rest, a willing medium waiting for the next collaborative endeavor. What next, indeed. The possibilities, and the stories, are endless.

Pictured: Fir, Tansy, October, Periwinkle, and Indigo. Mostly Merino: Merino Wool and Kid Mohair, 2-ply worsted weight. Hand-dyed by Margaret Klein Wilson. www.spinnery.com

Acknowledgments

We want to thank our invaluable interns from Mount Holyoke College, Amy Magiera, Allison Walacavage, and Jessica LaPointe, and our wonderful editors at Three Rivers Press, Becky Cabaza and Carrie Thornton (even if they wouldn't let us sneak in those extra words).

Contents

PREFACE XV

PART ONE **our people**

DOWN THE GENERATIONS: KNITTING FOR
(AND WITH) OUR YOUNG

Our Knitting Heroine • Stephanie Pearl-McPhee 3
Temporarily Almost a Blanket • Terry Miller Shannon 10
Babymaking • Kelly Elayne 12
Empty Blanket • Christie Nowak 16
Other Daughters • Laurie Doran 20
Knitting Daughters • Miriam Lang...23
A Goodly Heritage? • Janine Tinklenberg 26
Full Circle • Sheila Anderson 29

MATES: OUR BEST BELOVEDS (WELL, MOST OF THE TIME)

**I'm Gonna Sit Right Down and
   Knit Myself a Sweater** • Jody Kolodzey.....................................31
Italian Shells • Lorraine Lener Ciancio 32
A Good Fit • Jay Elliott..35
The Sweater • Charmian Christie..39
Some Things Just Go On and On • Abha Iyengar 43

My Wife Is a *Knitter:* A Triptych • Jef Buehler 47

The Bind-Off: A Knitting Mystery • Stephen D. Rogers 51

Real Men Knit • Dawn Goldsmith..54

Not Fair! • Christine Basham...57

SIDE BY EACH: FRIENDS, SIBS, COLLEAGUES

Three Little Kittens Summa Cum Laude • Nancy Clark 60

Grimace and Old Blue • Jenny Feldon 64

Aunt Shirley's Snow Families • Jean Stone................................68

Competitive Knitting • Beth Walker 71

The Live-Lobster Sweater • Suzanne Strempek Shea.................75

The Fort River Knitting Circle • Martie Stothoff.......................80

Knit TWO Together • Jeannine Bakriges.....................................82

Letter to My Sister • Janet Blowney 85

Sweaters from "The Keep" • Marge Wooley 89

The Artist • E. B. Clutter 91

THOSE WHO BORE AND NURTURED US:
FOREMOTHER KNITTING

Dropped Stitches • Helen Kay Polaski..95

The Pink Bikini • Tara Jon Manning...99

A Different Time • Kay Dorn 102

With Relish • Hannah Treworgy 105

The Reminder • Kathryn Eike Dudding 108

The Knitting Studio • Chris Mastin...111

Sweaters • Lesléa Newman 115

PART TWO things of the spirit

HARD TIMES: THROUGH THICK, THIN, AND BOUCLÉ

How I Learned to Knit • Kathy Myers..125

Peace Blanket • Kathryn Gunn 128

What Goes Around Comes Around • Sondra Rosenberg 130

To Knit or Not to Knit • Dana Snyder-Grant 133

The Whole World in My Hands • Dayna Macy 137

What Does Knitting Have to Do with War? • Nilda Mesa....................140

In the Void • Marie Dorian 143

What's Your Hobby? • Luke Shiffer..146

MUSINGS: THOUGHTS FLOW AS YARN FLOWS THROUGH THE FINGERS

The Precognitive Knitter • Stephen Mead 149

A Glossary of Knitting • Zoë Blacksin 150

Story of Fiber • Wren Ross 152

Tricoter • Jenny Frost 156

Fables for Knitters • Natalie Harwood.......................................159

UFOs: The Lesson of Imperfection • Susan Atkinson...............................161

The Great Unfinishable • Perri Klass 164

Villanelle for Anthony • Jamie McNeely.......................................169

CREATOR/CREATING/CREATIVE: KNITTING THE SPIRIT

A Psalm • Donna Jaffe...171

Prayer Shawls • Carole Ann Camp...172

Sweater Grace • Claudia Conner..176

The Sock Heel • Molly Wolf 180

Binding Off • Janis Leona 184

PART THREE stash

ODD BALLS: BITS FROM THE STASH

BEEPBEEPBEEP • Barbara Wagner 191

Not-Cleaning • Suzanne Cody 196

The Visit • Michael Learmond 198

Weinhardt • Nancy Huebotter 202

The Perfect Plan • Adrienne Martini................................206

Learning to Knit at Fifty • Christine Lavin........................210

FROM SHEEP TO SHAWL (OR, BAA, HUMBUG)

Hot Wire! • Rosanne Anderson...215

The Uneasy Fiber Source • Micki Smith 217

What Do You Do with a Dead Sheep? • Laurie Clark...............220

Fiber Addiction • Donna Nothe-Choiniere...........................223

THE STUFF OF THE MATTER: WOOL

Mariah Educates the Sensitive • Susan Blackwell Ramsey 229

Why I Spin • Deborah Robson 232

Incrementalism • Ellen de Graffenreid 234

A Rose by Any Other Name • Mari Jane Bartley 238

Stuffing • Rena Trefman Cobrinik.......................................242

In the Old Days • Marcy Moffet 247

Color Hunger • Betty Christiansen.......................................249

Cauldrons of Color • Janette Ryan-Busch 253

ABOUT THE EDITORS AND CONTRIBUTORS.......................257

Preface

"Oh, Linda! This is worse than walking into a yarn store!"

"Yeah, I know. There's just so *much* stuff. I don't know what to pick."

The looming stacks of stories on our desks approached avalanche point. Stories about sweaters, sheep, grandmothers, boyfriends, babies, 9/11, dyepots, knitting disasters—and then there were the poems, dozens of them. When we started to put together the first *KnitLit* book, we had about 150 pieces to choose from. This time, we had hundreds and hundreds. What's the old saying, "Nothing exceeds like excess"?

So we started sorting. The first cut is always the easiest: There are pieces that are clearly excellent, pieces that are clearly no-gos, and a lot of pieces in the middle. But the second cut, choosing from that huge middle lot, was murder. Imagine many anguished conversations between your editors: "But I really *love* this one!" "Yes, but we've already got seven others like that. . . ."

Making *KnitLit Too* was like designing a sweater from stash: You want to make it as varied as possible. We wanted stories from different places. We wanted stories by men as well as by women. We wanted stories to reflect more than the main

KnitLit themes of fiber obsession and warm, loving relationships; we wanted dark colors to set off lighter hues, for light needs darkness to make it shine. We wanted stories to reduce us to damp piles of goo and stories to make us laugh so hard we got the hiccups (and yes, we got both). We wanted earthy and classy, urban and rural, plain and fancy, sexy and sacred.

What we *didn't* want was what we got: having to make extremely tough judgment calls. (Hint to contributors: Molly is *much* more ruthless than Linda.)

But we made them, and then we did a word count.

No, said our publisher, you may not hand in an extra twenty thousand words. Uh-uh. No way.

Oh, phooey, we said. Or words to that effect.

More cutting. More pain. Necessity, they say, is the smother of intention.

Trust us, people, this book *should* be of Harry Potteresque length; it should be as fatly, richly, nobly rounded as an 8-ounce ball of pure merino worsted. But we have behaved ourselves and kept it to the promised length. (*Sigh.*)

Here it is. Enjoy! (You should have seen the ones that got away. . . .)

—Linda Roghaar and Molly Wolf

Our People
part one

IN WHICH WE TELL OF MATES, MOTHERS,
GRANDMOTHERS, CHILDREN, NIECES AND NEPHEWS,
GRANDCHILDREN, FRIENDS, COLLEAGUES—ALL THOSE
WITH WHOM WE ARE KNIT TOGETHER.

Down the Generations: Knitting for (and with) Our Young

Our Knitting Heroine

Stephanie Pearl-McPhee

Our knitting heroine is a Canadian. This means that she must skate, whether she likes it or not. Let us assume that in this case, the operative word is "not." She is, however, married to Darling, a Newfoundlander, and this means that the offspring of this union must skate, and often, and in inclement weather. Newfoundlanders are a hardy breed, and their only concession to the cold seems to be thrummed mittens. This particular Newfoundlander has yet to put on a hat or do up his coat this winter, despite severe cold. Our heroine only thanks her lucky stars every day that her children are girls, and she is thereby excused from taking them to hockey. (While girls are more than welcome to play hockey, it is still only mandatory for boys. With girls, people ask you if your girls play hockey, not on what team.)

It is Darling's life's work to teach our heroine to skate backward, as he considers this a vital skill. Our heroine does sometimes try to imagine the circumstances under which her life could be saved by skating backward. Thus far, she has not succeeded. Still, because she is eager to be a good mother, she skates, if only frontward and as infrequently as possible.

Let us imagine for a moment, then, that our heroine is going skating, since it is only -15°C (-25°C with windchill) and therefore "warm."*

Now, what would *you* do if you had to go somewhere you didn't want to go, in order to do something that you find boring—but that leaves your hands free?

Thank you for your instant understanding. Our heroine packed the bed socks that she's currently working on because they are on 6-millimeter plastic double-pointed needles that aren't likely to freeze to her fingers, as metal needles would.

When her skating party reaches the pond, dependable Darling ties up all their skates and they stand up to head for the ice. Our knitting heroine reaches into her backpack, assembles her knitting, tucks the ball of yarn into her coat pocket, and takes a step, airily acting for all the world like this is perfectly normal.

She glances at Darling and her girls. All four are struck speechless.

* Our knitting heroine, being Canadian, does degrees Celsius, and if she didn't, her mother would have something to say. For those of you south of the border, that's about 7°F. or -4°F. with windchill.

"You have got to be kidding me," says Darling, eloquent as always.

"Moth-ERRRR!" say the daughters.

Now, our heroine has faced criticism before. There are those who think her odd. But her love of knitting and lack of time to do it make her uniquely qualified to answer these concerns.

"What?" she asks blandly. She is going to slide this right past them. She is the queen of cool. They don't *know* what's normal for knitters, after all. Yes, this could be her being weird. It could also be what all knitters do in the winter. It's all a confidence thing.

"That can't be smart!" Darling replies. But he and our heroine have been together a long time, and he knows that she is not easily coerced. She can be tricked, but she can rarely be convinced to detour from her chosen path without a really good reason. Apparently "logic," "good sense," and "an impending sense of doom" are not really good reasons.

"Isn't this kind of like running with scissors?" her eight-year-old chimes, looking concerned; you can see her making a mental note to skate far away from her mother. *That's it, kid, bite that hand that feeds you.*

Our heroine smiles, brushing off the comment; mere child, what does she know?

Our heroine walks down to the ice. She's not really worried, not being one to cloud the issue with facts and logic. Still . . . this might be another one of those moments that, retroactively, she should have seen coming. Such things do happen. She decides to give the idea a second thought. There: second thought done. Skating and knitting seem a perfectly natural combination. After all, she can walk and knit at the same time, and she's skated enough that she's not likely to fall while knitting. She can knit socks without looking, so she can keep eyes front to avoid skewering people at random.

Furthermore (I'd like to point out that despite what happened later, our heroine *did* have a "furthermore," an indication that she really *had* thought this through) if she did fall, she was unlikely to run herself through with plastic 6-millimeter double-pointed needles. Just to make sure, she gives her coat a test poke with the needle.

Reassured that knitting while skating really was an idea whose time had come, she steps gracefully onto the ice and meanders around the edge, knitting away.

Now, with some stories, there is a moment where it all starts to go wrong—a moment when you look at the character and think, "Uh-oh" or "Look out behind you!" or "He's in the basement" or "For God's sake, don't go into the forest!" In this story, that moment is subtle. It is not obvious.

Our heroine reaches into her pocket to pull out another length of yarn.

This is when the ball of yarn falls out of her pocket.

It is acrylic yarn, chunky, white. Which is a shame, because if our heroine had been a huge fan of neon pink, she might still be welcome to go skating.

The aforementioned ball of yarn is on the ice, and our heroine is blithely skating away from it, still knitting merrily along. Darling, who (quite frankly) has just been itching for a reason to be right about knitting and skating, picks it up. Darling trails our heroine, about 15 feet away, holding the yarn aloft and making excellent points about how the yarn has got wet, and he knew something bad would happen, and didn't he tell her that this was a bad idea? Our heroine, chastened, is about to tell him that he is definitely right, and that this disaster could have been averted if only she had listened . . . when they simultaneously spot the trouble.

A small child, skating at the speed of light, is streaking toward the span of yarn that connects our heroine and Darling. Realizing that they are jointly going to clothesline the little sweetie, Darling lowers his end of the yarn, essentially turning the clothesline into a tripwire. (Why he didn't raise it above the kid's head has never been satisfactorily settled.) The kid hits the yarn (white on white, remember?) going about a zillion miles per hour. He falls down and begins a long slide.

Ever watch curling? No? How about bowling?

Our heroine's thirteen-year-old daughter is standing with a gaggle of her preteen friends about 10 feet off, trying to look cool (and succeeding, since they are all too cool to wear hats), oblivious to the child whom our heroine has innocently turned into a projectile.

They never see it coming. (Except for that perfect Brittany . . . how does she do it? All this, and shell-pink lip gloss too.) Helpless, our heroine and Darling watch the six-year-old spin as he slides. To her grave, our heroine will swear that he maneuvered himself so as to knock down as many of the girls as possible. The six-year-old hits the preteens the way a toddler hits the block tower his sister has been working on for the last two hours.

Our heroine and Darling gasp in horror. They rush toward the scene. As they do, our heroine skates to the left of her eleven-year-old and the eleven-year-old's buddy, and Darling goes around on their right. Our heroine is still holding her knitting, and Darling is still holding the ball of yarn. The eleven-year-old, like any child her age, loses interest as soon as she realizes that no one is really hurt, and she turns to skate away.

Little does she know that her loving parents have wrapped her skates in deadly yarn.

Since they have tied her left skate to the ice, she doesn't get too far. As their daughter heads iceward, she grabs her friend's arm, taking her with her.

It is at this point that our heroine realizes that days like this are probably why she isn't taken very seriously at school parent council meetings.

Badly rattled now, Darling and our heroine realize that he must hand her the yarn before they actually strangle someone. He glares at her as she takes the ball. Clearly, he thinks this is all her fault.

They crouch on the ice to tend to various shocked children. Our heroine puts her knitting down on the ice to brush snow off kids and to wave reassuringly at the stunned parents watching from the sidelines. She has to admit that she sympathizes with these parents. From their perspective it must have seemed that their children were thrown to the ground by a viciously wielded invisible force field.

Remarkably, none of the children is hurt. In fact, the projectile six-year-old looks dazzled. His comments cause our heroine to wonder if this episode has given him ideas for some G.I. Joe–style sabotage of his own.

"Was that on purpose?" he asks Darling, who is checking him over.

"No way," says Darling, who would never hurt a fly.

"It was pretty cool," says the six-year-old, and off he skates, clearly trying to figure out how he can do that all over again.

Darling stands and shakes the snow off his clothes. Our heroine can tell that he might be a little upset. It is not often that our heroine's knitting plans end with disaster on this scale. Her mind is racing. In her own defense, she'd like to point out that this is not solely her fault. If the yarn had been wool, not acrylic, it would have snapped long before it could have done that kind of damage; moreover, if it hadn't been white and perfectly camouflaged by the ice, the victims might have stood a chance. She pores over all of this in her mind. How could anyone predict something like this? Pulling herself together, she decides that her best defense is a good offense . . . she is going to point out, that despite the 3-foot height of the juvenile missile, Darling had opted to lower, not raise, the yarn. After all, if he had raised the yarn, none of this would have happened. Our heroine has now been knitting for thirty years, and this is the first time that nine people have been knocked over in under three minutes as a result of her habit. This (she plans to say) was a freak accident, and not anything that you could blame on her, or on knitting. It was an act of God, like a tornado, a flood. It says nothing about combining knitting with skating. If people had given up trying to make planes when the first one didn't fly . . . well, where would humanity be? Finally (she intends to say) innovation and the creative spirit are often unconventional. You have to try new things to stay young. . . .

She is going to tell Darling all this when suddenly he is no longer in front of her. He is down on the ice. He has tried to skate over her knitting, which she has forgotten to pick up.

She picks it up now, and humbly goes to sit in the car.

Temporarily Almost a Blanket

Terry Miller Shannon

My niece is expecting a son. Sarah's highly anticipated little boy is causing my fingers to itch and tingle. And so I dig out my knitting book. I find my yarn—just as I did while looking forward to each of my grandbabies. It's actually the same blue-pink-yellow variegated yarn I stitched then, and also while awaiting a few other infants. The roughly rolled balls, knit and unraveled repeatedly, yield a strand as squiggly as my handwriting. It is a script that tells a tale. Some might call the plot of the story "the short-lived triumph of hope over experience and common sense." But to me, it's quite a different yarn.

That evening when Craig starts telling me something, I raise my eyebrows without lifting my eyes. I bob my head in what the husband of any knitter translates as, "In a second, babe. I'm counting."

When I'm done, I say, "Sorry. I was casting on."

"Sarah's baby?"

"Yep. Blanket, of course."

His eyebrows stitch together. "*Again?* What say we cut directly to the chase right now and go buy her a baby book instead? Or a nice store-bought comforter?"

"It's not the baby blanket that's important," I say, my fingers wrapping yarn and pulling stitches through loops. "It's the tradition."

In the evenings while Craig watches TV, I listen, with my eyes glued to my yarn and needles.

"Will you look at that," Craig says.

"I can't." I concentrate. Knit one. Purl one. "I've got to watch what I'm doing. You know."

Boy, does he know. I can knit like crazy. Purling is no problem. What I can't do is fix my mistakes. One little misstep and I'm done. I have to rip the entire project out. My lack of recovery adds a thrill of suspense that most knitters probably don't experience.

But I love the stitching. In the rhythmic click of needles, my mind takes a holiday. I hold my infant grandchildren for the first time once again, jolted by a weird lightning flash of recognition when I gaze into their blue eyes. My sons time-warp to the past, shrinking to warm powder-sweet bundles, with tiny starfish hands. And then I remember other babies I've cuddled, including my now-expectant niece, Sarah—her small flower face bright beneath an amazing cap of thick dark hair. And then, further back, my parents settle Sarah's mom into my three-and-a-half-year-old big-sister lap on the day I meet my baby sister.

"Still knitting?" Craig asks periodically.

"Look." I display the short length of blanket hanging from my knitting needles, marveling at the transformation of yarn to fabric.

Then, one night it happens. "Uh-oh. Oh. No."

"Dropped a stitch?"

I nod. My knitting book falls open at a touch to "How to Pick Up a Dropped Stitch," which might as well be written in Swahili for all the good it does me. I halfheartedly pick around at the loops with the tip of my knitting needle. But I know the jig is up.

"UPS it to your mom," Craig suggests. "She can fix it and send it back to you."

But there's no need to fix the error. I never expect to actually complete a baby blanket. As always, my needlework has done its intended job—time-traveled me back to my life's sweet baby times. Made me anticipate nuzzling Sarah's little Bayden when he arrives. The blanket I've knit deep within, out of elusive threads of soft memories and bright dreams, may be invisible, but it will never stop warming me.

"So . . . a nice baby book, you think?" I pull the yarn from the dwindling blanket in smooth, well-practiced strokes, feeling as refreshed as if I've just risen from my hammock on a beach.

Craig nods. He fingers the kinky strands squiggling between us. "Ever think of throwing this stuff out? It's been knit and unraveled into oblivion."

"Never," I say. And I roll the yarn up for next time.

Babymaking
Kelly Elayne

It is raining in Southern California.

This is an aberration and I am inconsolable. It is a Saturday, it is raining, and I am single.

It is officially a good day to knit.

I head into the infamous Valley below sky-hung drapes of gray wetness, maneuvering my car through a sea of Volvos down the infinite Ventura Boulevard to a yarn shop reminiscent of a French café: La Knitterie Parisienne.

The name makes one imagine butter-soaked pastries and complicated caffeinated brews. Instead, each time I visit, I find a warm den of dimly lit shelves, their cubicles stuffed with yarn. In my soggy hands, I have one of my current projects: inches of hand-dyed mohair rows I hope will someday bloom into a scarf. I carry the project in La Knitterie's signature glossy black bag with its logo scripted across the face.

A bell above the shop door tinkles, announcing my arrival, and heads turn, damp from the rain like mine. They greet me with smiles, welcome me into a haven of femininity, domesticity, and contentment. Past the first few aisles of yarn, off to the right, there is an oval table surrounded by cushioned chairs. Four women sit casually blending needles and yarn in a hum of quiet conversation and muted clicking. I reserve a seat with my purse and today's knitting assignment, safe and dry in its glossy bag, then tiptoe off to shop.

I must confess . . . today's assignment is yesterday's assignment, last week's assignment, and last month's assignment. It is last year's assignment.

I have this uncontrollable habit of starting but never finishing a single knitted piece. It must be the grand selection of yarn, the plethora of needles, my intolerance for imperfections. I must buy more, start more, dream more, knit more. But when I find a dropped stitch I must stop, disassemble, and recast. If an edge starts to curl I must stop, disassemble, and recast. At this rate, I will never finish anything. Buy more yarn, must buy more yarn, imagining this pink or that pink in baby booties, even though I have no boyfriend.

And then there's my green tweed suit with the tan buttons; I want to knit a camisole thingy to wear with it. Drifting up and down aisles, I squeeze skeins, pull imported bundles from their cubbies, search for some tranquil fusion of mint green and caramel-taupe. The selection is intimidating; some yarns are so precious and in such short supply you have to talk yourself out of buying them. Only enough to knit one sock, only enough to yearn for more.

Women float by me with pregnant bellies and dripping raincoats, humming nursery rhymes or comparing labels or mumbling to themselves about that or another divine design, calculating gauge. They have finished many things. They fill their baskets with twisted skeins and pattern books of windswept cheeks and toothy smiles covered in handknit possibilities.

This one has knitted her newborn a receiving blanket with a bath cloth to match. They browse the button aisle ruminating over hand-painted animals, marble disks, and bamboo adornments. That one has knitted her three-year-old a smock to wear over her play clothes. They have finished many things.

The aroma of dusty synthetics and musty wool tickles my nose; microscopic filaments of thread make me sniffle and occasionally sneeze. I run my fingers over colors that charm me, feeling glamorous silkiness or rugged knobbiness. I settle on a combed mohair similar to the yarn I brought with me, but more refined, tie-dyed in yellow, mauve, and baby blue. I eye a pair of knitting needles at the register. Made more for looks than technique, they are carved from birch, stained and lacquered, smooth as glass chopsticks, with fluted ends like candlesticks. The salesclerk wraps my purchase in another glossy black tote.

And now it's time to knit.

This is what I love about La Knitterie, this table of women joined in a circle, intertwined: fingers flashing, yarn unfurling, wood or metal needles skipping and dipping and tucking, pouring out patterns of useful order and comfort. I seat myself among them, stretch out my scarf-to-be, still just a lazy spool of mohair loom-spun by Renaissance Faire players. Hot red flashes with cobalt blue and gold, sticky and untidy in a mass of knotted plushness; I pull off several arms' lengths, lay them loosely atop the mass, then release my needles, beige plastic number 13s, from their neon point protector. I thrust my needle under the first stitch, loop fresh yarn over, slide everything off, and repeat over and over again until a rhythm takes hold, casual yet meticulous, birthing a rectangle of mathematically symmetrical loops.

As I get into the groove, I glance at the women around me; they wear half-smiles, their drifting eyes count stitches, their finished fabric covers bellies brewing infants ready to wear, ready to soil, ready to nest. Some knit fast and determinedly, others slowly and gently. Our minds meet somewhere in midair, clicking and counting and tugging at yarn until it seems as if the table itself is one great sweater we are all knitting together.

I revel in the gracefulness of it, the precision of my needles guiding the yarn as though I'm decorating a wedding cake with pipings of fuzzy frosting.

The bell above the shop door tinkles. We all look up, smile, nod our heads hello to the damp-headed newcomer. Classical music tinkles through the shop's stereo system, rain tinkles against the glass-front windows, needles tinkle against wedding rings and manicured nails.

And then it hits me. I've been working on three different scarves for more than a year, never finishing anything, only knitting in this blissful rhythm, because it's not about the scarves or the socks or the hats. It's not about the sweaters and the shawls and the blankets.

It is about the act of knitting.

It's about joining two elements in the simplest of forms incrementally. It's about tiny cells multiplying into complicated structures. It's about this warmth expanding in my lap like a growing embryo. It's about emulating the rituals of motherhood, satisfying my feminine urge to create.

That's why I'm here. That's it.

Empty Blanket
Christie Nowak

We chatted with brittle gaiety about inconsequentials as we found our seats and stowed our gear, rehashing old conversations. By now, I knew exactly what Mike was going to eat for breakfast and precisely how long Mom was planning to sleep. They both were left with no doubt as to my plans for the too-tight dress pumps I'd been wearing all week. Equally well known, but carefully unmentioned, were all the things we'd miss most about Guatemala—gooey fried plantains, warm October sunshine, soft baby skin.

Baby skin. I took a fast, deep breath and shook my head fiercely, damming the reservoir of tears again. I cursed my shoes for emphasis and clicked my seat belt into place. Then I looked up.

They were both staring at me, dangerously silent, deeply worried. I groped for a new topic of distraction, but none came.

"Christie?" Mom asked, as Mike grabbed my hand.

I slammed my eyes shut on their anxiety. "No tears," I whispered, a soul-strengthening mantra. "Not yet."

The intercom let loose a burst of rapid Spanish and our flight attendants began their preflight pantomime. It gave all three of us a chance to plug the holes in our personal dikes.

Images of little fingers poking through little holes brought to mind my blanket, tucked safely in the bag under the seat, as it had been on my way down. It took up most of the room in the diaper-bag-turned-carry-on that I'd bought in May, leaving just barely space for my journal and for exposed film. But that was all right by me. After all, a carry-on is for those items you can't bear to be parted from if your luggage were to take a vacation without you. Usually, I cart around extra cash, my camera, maybe a change of underwear. But for this trip, nothing was more vital than that blanket.

The flight attendants, perfect smiles pasted onto perfect faces, were performing their synchronized seat-belt ballet when my resolve collapsed. Before the exit signs were fully illuminated, I'd reached beneath the seat and dragged my blanket into my lap. I needed it too much.

The engines rumbled awake, a pair of grouchy giants, and

the plane lurched away from the terminal. I fondled the folds of the blanket, remembering all the work I'd put into it, from studying knitting books for the ideal pattern to combing crafts stores for the sweetest yarn. I'd desperately wanted my first blanket to be perfect—a light, airy afghan with fancy stitches, but simple enough for a novice to master. And the yarn had to be kitten soft and little-boyish, neither too dark nor too pale. At last I'd found a downy baby-weight in white with light blue speckles. After many hours and more than the occasional ripping out, I'd turned that yarn into a lacy, rippled, crib-sized blanket for my son.

That project kept me sane through the long months of waiting. Whenever the tension of another administrative delay became too much to bear, I'd get a desperate grip on my needles and start to stitch. For the first twenty rows, I dreamed of my very first Mother's Day. May flew past. I completed the first half, promising to turn my mother into a grandmother for her birthday. June vanished. Finishing more rows, I watched parents on my street light fireworks for their children. July melted away. The next third of the blanket absorbed my dreams of frolicking with my child at my in-laws' summer cottage on the lake. August crept along. I cast off the final stitches to delivery room tales, told around a Labor Day picnic table.

All those stitches. All those empty months.

Since its completion, my blanket had lain alone in my son's crib. Not gathering dust—no, never gathering dust. I visited it every day, picked it up, held it to my face, kissed it, and tucked it in again. Every day. Until we got the call last week telling us we could finally go visit our baby. We couldn't bring him home yet, but after six months, a visit was a blessing. I'd finally be able to hold him, kiss him, and tuck him in.

What a joy that flight was. What sweet anticipation. We all felt it, running on the adrenaline of joy for the thirty-six hours it took to buy tickets, pack, board, fly, and finally settle into our hotel room with a soon-to-be-filled crib.

Now that crib was empty again, or perhaps already filled with another baby, watched furtively by another couple who waited in agony for a judge to sign his name and make them a family. But for a short time—just as we had—they'd have a few tantalizing, magical, never-to-be-forgotten days with the child of their hearts.

Or perhaps their judge has already signed, making their lives whole again. Maybe when they fly out of this very airport, their blanket will not be empty.

The growing engine noise covered my sobs as the dam finally crumbled. Mike hugged me tight, and our shoulders shook together. Over the engine's whine, I could hear my mother whisper, "Next time. Next time." She made it a prayer.

Our plane lifted from the ground, and my tears fell. I clung to my son's blanket. Would he remember me when I came back for him? Or would his trip home be a frightening journey into uncertainty? As my tears soaked into the blue and white yarn, I prayed that against all odds, he would somehow remember this blanket. His blanket. A blanket that now finally smells not of me, but of my baby.

Other Daughters
Laurie Doran

Last July, atop the highest mountain in the Northeast, I became a mother for the first time. Here's how it happened.

The store where I work hired Liz, a high school student, to work part-time. Throughout the year Liz and I chatted about our interests. Liz was curious about my mountain-climbing adventures. She was enthralled by my stories.

One day in early summer, after Liz had graduated from high school, she said, "My goal is to climb Mount Washington before I start college this fall. Will you lead me?"

A chill ran up my spine. This climb had been my dream, too, when I was Liz's age, but severe asthma had stopped me from trying it then. Now, old enough to be Liz's mother, I was thrilled to be asked to help this young woman reach her goal. Immediately I agreed.

This was Liz's first major climb. I wanted her to be properly prepared for this venture. I taught her what to take and how to load her pack.

After a three-hour drive, we reached the parking lot at the base of the mountain just before dawn. In the quiet of a brilliantly rosy sunrise, we shouldered our packs and headed up the broad rocky trail. We strolled beneath a canopy of green leaves, breathing in the cool morning air, hiking in rhythm, an unspoken bond between us as we watched gold sunlight filtering through the trees.

There it was: the headwall. I relied on my climbing experience to lead us up this narrow, vertical trail with sudden drops of several hundred feet. Close to the edge, I caught Liz as her foot slipped on the four-foot-high rock ledge. Hiding a sudden spurt of fear, I remembered something that I didn't tell Liz: A young man had slipped and fallen to his death at this very spot. I urged Liz to try it again and she succeeded. Our bond of trust grew deeper the higher we climbed.

We were halfway up the headwall, with more challenges still ahead. "If the wind picks up and dark clouds roll in, we'll turn around and go down Lion's Head Trail," I said. She nodded.

The boulder-strewn trail ahead tugged us upward. The last mile of our trip would be steep, rocky, and exposed to weather. Liz, tall and slender, reveled in the high-altitude dance, hopping from boulder to boulder. I plodded. At last we climbed the 100 stairs to the top of the mountain 6,288 feet above sea level.

The summit was crowded with visitors of all ages milling about, enjoying the view. As we gazed out at the gray-blue peaks marching toward the horizon, Liz hugged me and whispered, "Will you be my mom?"

I choked with emotion and felt my eyes sting with tears. No one has ever called me "Mom." I simply nodded. Now that I was a mom, I said, "Congratulations on a job well done. Remember this day. Mountain climbing prepares you to deal with life. Go forward, pursue your dreams, and live well."

She smiled.

I knew this trip would prepare my "daughter" well for college. She would be leaving in a month. Already I was beginning to feel the pangs of the empty nest syndrome. I worried about where she'd be living, what courses she'd be taking, whether she'd have all the school supplies and clothes she needed.

It was then that I remembered the time when I'd left home for college. That summer, I watched my mother knit me a beautiful red sweater. This special gift was her way of sending me out into the world, wrapped in her love. Many times during that first semester at school, whenever I felt insecure and homesick, I'd wear that sweater. Snug and warm, I'd feel a link to my mom and home, where love resided.

My daughter, I sensed, felt the same uneasiness I had experienced about going away to college. She said, "Mom, I don't have enough clothes. Do you have something in your closet that would fit me?"

It made me proud to know that I could give my daughter the gift my mother had given me—a handknit sweater. I pulled out my most precious one, a crewneck pullover modeled on textiles worn by Byzantine royalty. As soon as I'd seen that pattern in *Stitches in Time*, I knew I *had* to knit that sweater. I'd combed through yarn stores searching for exactly the right weight and colors of yarn: cream, cranberry, black, olive green, navy blue, a touch of goldenrod yellow, a hint of peach. One sleeve was knit in cream, but the other was a complicated mosaic design of rectangles and squares. The body of the sweater had challenged my knitting skills. Inside each background color (and they changed frequently) danced intricate color patterns.

Now, as I smoothed out the soft, intricate folds, I imagined all the thoughts that my mother had knitted into my red sweater. Now I fully understood the meaning behind it. I wanted my daughter to take this sweater, her handknit treasure that I had created, off to college, knowing that even though she would be far away, we could still be close.

My daughter waltzed around the room holding the sweater in her arms. "Put it on," I said excitedly. She slipped the sweater over her head. And there was the magic.

It fit her perfectly! The sleeves and body length were just right. Her face glowed against the colors of the design. It seemed as though I had made the sweater especially for her. Strange, that I hadn't known her when I created it.

I am blessed by this daughter of mine, this daughter of my heart. And there will be other sweaters that I will knit for her, twining in love with each and every stitch, strengthening this bond that both of us have chosen.

Knitting Daughters
Miriam Lang

I have three sons, and I love them dearly. But although I have swathed them since birth in handknit rompers, booties, hats, sweaters, scarves, mittens and whatnot, not one of them has been much interested in learning to knit himself. So I have had to borrow other people's daughters. This has worked out remarkably well, if I do say so myself.

Leah, my first knitting daughter, had a terrible time getting started. Our sessions were frequently interrupted by tears— not all of them hers—as her doll's scarf had to be ripped out and reknitted. She was a persevering child, however, and unbelievably determined. She worked her way through the tangles and finished that damned scarf and moved on to more complicated projects. Eventually she graduated as the valedictorian of her high school class. Although I probably shouldn't take much of the credit for that, I think it's pertinent that her graduation speech was an allegory likening life to the knitting process. I was quite proud of her. She's at Princeton now, majoring in philosophy, math, and psychology—rather like knitting in three colors, I suppose.

My second knitting daughter, Deborah, has a more scientific bent. Or it could be that I'd become more analytical about the physical properties of knitting by the time I taught her. Whatever the reason, Deborah latched on to the patterns the stitches formed and extrapolated from them some fancy theories about pattern making in the natural world. Her paper describing her experiments with genetic engineering, in which she bred young fruit trees to espalier themselves up garden walls, won her one of those Westinghouse Competition Awards. You may have seen her on the *Today* show looking very fetching in an Aran Isle dress knit entirely from fibers extracted from the inner bark of trees. And all because I taught her to knit. Think of it.

Judith, my third knitting daughter, shares my love of literature. We talk a lot about books while we knit together. In fact, there's a logical relationship between the books and the knitting. We've worked our way from a discussion of unintended consequences in *Holes*, by Louis Sachar, to the passive-aggressive machinations of that famous knitter Madame Defarge in Dickens's *A Tale of Two Cities*. Just last summer, Judith, who's a pretty persuasive character herself, raised more than $33,000 for the local library by selling lemonade and handknit bookmarks down at the train station. Not bad for a ten-year-old.

And my boys? I won't say they've been wholly unaffected by all the knitting going on around them. Consider this: Any knitter can recognize the similarity between the language of knitting patterns and the binary code in which computers communicate. All those 0s and 1s might just as well be knits and purls, right? Well, Nathaniel, my oldest, was besotted with computer code at a tender age. And I like to think that it was all my muttering about poorly translated knitting patterns that influenced his ability to crack arcane computer codes. He can't tell us much about the work he's doing for the UN, but he assures us it's to aid world peace. Let's hope.

And the middle boy, Sam, was recently featured on National Public Radio for having invented the word *disacuate*, meaning "to lose a needle." It's unlikely that this contribution to the English language would have occurred outside the home of a knitter. Though now that I stop to think of it, his father, who is a surgeon, probably has equal claim as an inspiration. Still, I'd rather disacuate in among the sofa cushions than in a patient, wouldn't you?

My third boy, Jeremiah, is primarily interested in baseball at the moment. Last season we worked out a few rudimentary signs for use while I'm knitting in my strategically placed lawn chair down the third-base line—unobtrusive signs, like sticking my needles through the ball of yarn when the steal is on or flourishing a cable needle when a bunt is in order. It amused us no end to watch the opposing teams trying to steal signs from our decoy third base coach's meaningless gestures. We won our division last year and we're hoping to make it to the state championships next season. We still have the rest of the winter to improve on our system.

Useful stuff, knitting.

A Goodly Heritage?

Janine Tinklenberg

I have taught my daughters to knit . . . and lived to regret it.

I admit it: One of the reasons I wanted daughters was so I could pass down this goodly heritage to them. I had this hazy dream that life would be perfect: me with my knitting and a daughter or two arrayed beside me, solemnly and quietly knitting away. This dream, like so many ill-conceived notions of parenting, was to die a slow death by reality.

I did, with my husband's help, manage the daughter part. In fact, we managed it twice. All that remained was to teach them the knitting part. I bought a pair of needles and a ball of yarn for my older daughter when she was only three. She thought it mighty amusing when she could "knit" along with Mommy by sticking her needles into the yarn and wiggling them. Her efforts at knitting lasted about five minutes before she got bored and wandered off. I bided my time.

Five years later, trapped at Urgent Care with her one Sunday afternoon with nothing else to do, I sat her down beside me, handed her a circular needle and some bulky red yarn, and taught her yet again to knit. It seemed like a good idea at the time. Daughter number one proudly displayed her inch or two of gnarled and knotty doll scarf. The nurses *oohed* and *aahed*, amazed that a child her age could knit.

Daughter number two swiftly followed her sister's example. The two girls now adore knitting. Each has her own knitting bag with needles, yarn, and a knitting doll.

It's awful.

It's not that I don't think that they should knit. I remember learning to knit when I was around eight years old, and I am glad they're interested.

I just wish they wouldn't knit when *I* knit.

Huh?

Well, it's like this: My knitting is my refuge from a world of frustration. It comes in handy when I am feeling flustered. Many a cooking disaster, many a tiff with the spouse, get smoothed away through knitting. But now, when I sit down to work out my frustration by knitting, I am immediately joined by two little girls who say, "Oh, I'm going to get my knitting, too!"

How sweet, I can hear you thinking. Yep, I thought it was sweet too, those first few times. And it would be sweet, if they actually *knit* in these sessions.

Instead, what they really do is make a lot of mistakes. Just when I'm hitting the zone, soothing away my cares and trouble with the application of yarn and needles, the first little voice sounds.

"Mommy," the voice says, "can you fix this? I don't know what I did, but this big loop is hanging off!" Ah. The child had slipped five stitches, turned the needles around and knit backward for two stitches, and then dropped one stitch and knit with the tail for six more. There; mistake fixed.

Just when my needles have managed to spirit me back into that place where there is no cooking or cranky spouses but only the knitted fabric building slowly beneath my hands, the other daughter says, "What do I do again after I put the needle in the loop?" I try patiently to show her, but her eyes have drifted to the television set where Teletubbies are cavorting on the screen, raptly watched by her brother. "Look," I say. "Look at what I'm doing!" Daughter drags her eyes away from the screen and gives me a blank stare. I say again, "Look, in through the front door, run around the back, down through the window, off jumps Jack!"—the classic knitting rhyme, which I have now recited for the (at least) one hundredth time. Daughter takes back her knitting, mumbling her thanks, eyes straying back to the screen. "Oh, no!" Dipsy says. "Run away!" My sentiments exactly.

Our cozy knitting session continues on in this vein, a sort of weird tennis match ensuing. We pass yarn and needles back and forth, child making mistake after mistake and mother correcting them all, until my own knitting ends up back in my bag and I seek refuge elsewhere in the house, growling softly to myself.

Someday I know I will be glad that I taught them. Truly. I mean it. They will think back to their childhood and reverently remember, "My mom taught me how to knit!" I will be glad . . . then.

As for now, I have become a secret knitter, a closet knitter, a knitter waiting for children to go to bed, go to school, go outside, go anywhere, just so long as I can sneak my needles out of my bag and get back to that soothing rhythm that makes life whole again.

Full Circle

Sheila Anderson

With number 12 needles cast on,
in baby pinkest 3-ply yarn,
to knit a new creation.

Increase one stitch at each end
of every week until full term.
Give birth to a tiny garment,
sewn together with loving care,
Then continue to increase its size,
using a slightly thicker ply
of rosier hue, but never
quite cutting the maternal cord.

Continue in stocking stitch each year,
until required length is reached.
Maintain this size by following the same pattern.
Take time to pick up any dropped stitches
and to correct any mistakes.
Although (please note) the finished garment
may stretch out of shape over time.

Wash garment gently on wool cycle,
taking extra care as it grows old and worn.
Expect the parts to shrink with age,

to wrinkle and turn gray, and for
the pattern style to date.

Begin decreasing as the garment
nears its end. Cast off loosely.

Age-spotted, paper thin, and limp,
our garment's served its purpose.
The moths and years have eaten their fill;
it is quite ready to unravel at the seams.
Pull back the rows, unwind
each memory line by line.
Roll up a life's experience
into a smooth round ball.

Recycle into 3-ply yarn,
and tint a delicate baby pink.
With number 12 needles cast on . . .

Mates: Our Best Beloveds (Well, Most of the Time)

I'm Gonna Sit Right Down and Knit Myself a Sweater

Jody Kolodzey

Sung to the tune of
"I'm Gonna Sit Right Down and Write Myself a Letter,"
by Fred E. Ahlert and Joe Young

I'm gonna sit right down and knit myself a sweater
And make believe it came from you.
I'll make popcorn stitches so neat,
They'll look good enough to eat.
A lot of cables on the bottom,
I know how to plot 'em.

I'm gonna thread the neckline with a piece of leather
And knot the ends the way you do.
I'm gonna sit right down and knit myself a sweater
And make believe it came from you.

[Instrumental break]
[Repeat]

Italian Shells
Lorraine Lener Ciancio

We celebrated my thirty-ninth birthday in Ostia, half an hour by train from Rome. On a night in August in the walled courtyard of a small family restaurant, my lover and I ordered a *grande* bottle of *vino russo* to go with *frito misto*, sautéed eggplant, and other delicacies I cannot now recall. We tried to tell the owner's daughter that it was my birthday we were celebrating, but our British phrase book lacked the right Italian term: *compleanno*. Sea breezes filled the air with salty dampness, mingling with the kitchen scents of garlic, roasted peppers, and olive oil. Christmas lights in the old trees and candles on the rough wooden tables provided the only light.

More than twenty years later, my husband and I can still recall almost every detail of that trip to Italy. We are both Italian-Americans. Like most of our people, if someone asks about our nationality, we always say "Italian"—acknowledging not a conscious decision, but a spirit that exists beyond us.

Much of Italy, now as well as then, takes August off. We found many of the shops and sights in Rome were *chiuso*, closed for the long summer holiday—even the Sistine Chapel. And so we fled the city, taking the train to Rome's closest seaside resort, and found a room in a hotel near the beach. Now, on my *compleanno*, we slowly explored the back streets and cafés of Ostia. The town is known for its black-sand beaches and for ancient ruins rivaling Pompeii's; back in 1979, they were just beginning to be excavated.

We found ourselves drawn toward the crowded Lido di Ostia, where families were enjoying their August vacations. Along the lido, vendors sold everything from drinks and sweets to souvenirs and T-shirts. Pausing at the cart of an old woman wearing a flowery cotton dress and white sneakers, we dawdled, turning over the eye-catching seashells. She spoke no English and we knew only a little Italian, but we managed to negotiate the purchase of the half-dozen or so shells that most appealed to us. While my lover counted out lire, the woman handed me a sea green shell as a gift, took my hand in hers, looked at both of us, and said with a smile, "*Amore.*"

As a knitter, I am always lured by color, texture, romance. During my younger years, I often started projects based solely on emotion. Before our trip, back home in the coastal town in Connecticut where I lived, I had been working on a thick, tweedy gray-and-yellow pullover for my lover and had finished all but the sleeves—the critical place in knitting where I often ran out of enthusiasm and put projects aside with a guilt-ridden permanence. I already had a few unfinished sweaters in a box in the attic. But this one was different. This one was for *him*.

At the last moment before we left for the airport, I stashed the needles, some hastily jotted pattern notes, and a ball of yarn at the bottom of my suitcase. Somehow they represented a connection at once intimate and traditional, a connection I wanted to take with me to Italy. Of course, once we arrived in Rome, I never gave the sweater another thought. The balmy days and nights were too crammed with romance and food, new sights and sounds, to think about knitting.

When we returned to New England and our respective homes and jobs, I finished the sweater and presented it with a mixture of pride and relief.

But my head was still filled with a palette of hues and experiences from the journey. I longed to knit a sweater the color of the seashell that now sat on my desk near the typewriter. Once in a while, I'd pick it up and hold it to my ear. I never heard the sound of waves that shells are supposed to hold, nor did I smell salt water. But holding the shell evoked the emotions, tastes, and images I remembered from Ostia: the dark gray beach, the honky-tonk amusement park, the sidewalk cafés, the people spilling out onto the roads and blocking traffic at lunchtime.

For a while, I looked in vain for the exact color lodged in my mind—a faded blue-green, like old glass or sea water, but brighter. But, in time, the everyday tasks of career and motherhood and the prospect of marriage took over my life. The desire for a sweater made from yarn that reminded me of love and seashells slipped away. In fact, I stopped knitting for several years.

Recently, while browsing the shelves of a yarn shop in New Mexico, where I now live, I came across that elusive color. I wasn't looking for it—I hadn't even thought about it in years.

But there it was, taking me back to a few idyllic days in a tacky seaside resort in Italy. With the memories came a wistful recognition of time and youth gone by.

My lover/husband never wore the gray-and-yellow sweater I knitted for him. He admitted that when I began knitting it, he didn't want to hurt my feelings by telling me about his severe allergy to wool and his deep hatred of pullover sweaters, especially bulky ones. It stayed in a drawer for a few years, carefully folded and cared for, neither of us willing to admit that he would never put it on. One day, muttering the words "when in doubt, throw out," I ruthlessly stuffed it into a bag of clothing destined for the secondhand shop. Perhaps someone is contentedly wearing it now.

I wonder if that person sometimes has mystifying visions of a seaside resort, a place he or she has never visited.

A Good Fit
Jay Elliott

During my midfifties, I found myself undergoing a sort of physical and emotional renaissance. "Do you want to meet someone?" a friend asked, nudging me significantly. "Um, sure," I replied, trying to display nonchalance.

"Here's a number. You've got lots in common. She works with books, too."

With some trepidation—what the hell was I doing back in

the dating game after forty years?—I called. She had a warm voice, full of laughter. The conversation was promising: *Cool*, I thought. "Let's do lunch," I ventured.

I misjudged the traffic, of course, and arrived twenty minutes late, puffing and full of prepared excuses. But when I saw her rise from the table where she'd been waiting, I saw a wonderful big smile, with a hint of dimples that charmed me. It was early summer, and she was wearing a long, light, open jacket that flowed gracefully like chiffon and spoke of airy breezes. *Hmmm*, I thought. *This might work, if first impressions can be trusted.* She only let me get into the first of my "sorry I'm late" excuses and then we were right back in the conversation we'd had on the phone. Two hours slipped by without my knowing it.

Yes, we were both into books—I taught them, she sold them—and we could begin on that basis. We had both been married twice; her daughters were grown, safely through the teen years that my son was just embarking on. We wandered down intertwining conversational paths, completely at ease.

As we ordered our coffee (she took it black and unsugared, as I did), I leaned back a little, thinking that this was working better than I could ever have expected. Then, she leaned forward, fixing me with her charming smile. Her mild blue eyes took on a bit of the glazed quality of the newly converted. "Do you happen to knit?" she asked. Oops. "Uh, well, no," I stammered. For the first time during the lunch, I was nonplussed. How could she have figured I would know anything about knitting? Knitting's geeky, not sophisticated.

I had a momentary flash of memory, to a time in my adolescence when I'd been laid up with a broken arm and my aunt had taught me to knit. My plaster-constricted fingers had made the task frustrating and, to my mind, useless. Besides, what I'd wanted to do was to play baseball. The only thing that made the experiment even slightly bearable was listening to San Francisco Giants games during the lazy summer afternoons. *No, knitting is for grannies,* I thought to myself, *and for pregnant women with hair pulled tightly back into a bun, thick glasses drooping over their noses, and for earthy-crunchy types living on a limited hippie budget.*

Yet here was this attractive, accomplished, vibrant woman asking if I knew how to knit—and betraying, moreover, symptoms of passionate advocacy. "I learned how once," I said, to be saying something, anything. "But that was a long time ago. I have no idea any more what a knit is, let alone a purl. Besides," I confessed in a rush, "all I yearned for the whole time I was forced to knit was to play baseball. And I couldn't."

She put her head a little to one side and inspected me over the lifted coffee cup. It was an appealing gesture. "Someone told me once that your hands always remember," she said. I held up my hands, looked at them, and shook my head. "Nope," I said. "Not these." I recalled a *People* magazine headline I'd scanned waiting in the grocery line: KNITTING IS THE NEW YOGA! Something about how knitting leads to contemplation and exploring one's inner being. Or maybe it was the *National Enquirer.* I give both about equal credence. I remember thinking at the time that if knitting, of all things, could become part of our new-agey culture, then maybe baseball could as well. I conjured up a meeting on the mound. Manager: "Your karma a little out of sync today, Roy? That why they're hitting all those bullets off you? Maybe you should avail yourself of healing vibrations in the hot tub. Re-establish your basal rhythms." But *was* knitting getting chic? Was I suffering from contempt prior to investigation? In smugly adhering to my ironclad adolescent conclusion, was I, at my own peril, blatantly ignoring the rising cachet attached to the skill? And, just possibly, could this adamant refusal to change my opinion be a source of some of my interpersonal problems?

The upshot of the lunch, despite this turn of the conversation, was that we did keep seeing each other. I began to grow accustomed to having her knit beside me as I drove. She would knit as we sat beside each other at town functions or when we watched baseball games. I on the couch, she in her chair, bag on the floor, balls of yarn bouncing off the table, describing a soft arc like unto the line drives I was urging for the scarlet-hosed batters. More serendipity: She'd been raised a Red Sox fan, and I'd switched allegiance from the Giants to the Olde Town Team when I'd spent the summer of '67— "The Impossible Dream"—in Cambridge, between graduate school semesters. Now, as the Red Sox once again spiraled themselves out of play-off contention, she gave me a present: an alpaca scarf. Oh, it was soft, and I had to admit that the subdued and gentle blues and soft grays felt good nestled around my neck in the cold New England weather. It was a marker, I felt; a sign that things were going well.

Spring was in the offing, and she was off to a sheep and wool show. She gave me one of those sidelong looks I've come to know as the prelude to a knitting observation: "You need a vest for next fall." Measurements and pattern followed; I even accompanied her to the festival to help pick out the yarn— merino, this time. It turned out trim, comfortable, and (I have to admit) not as geeky as I thought it would be. Ever so slowly, the firm ground of my former observations about knitting was undergoing a radical shift; I even picked up some of the jargon, like *increase* and *decrease* and *yarnover*, if not the actual activities. I visited my own apartment less and less, wondering if I was paying rent for a mail drop only. We agreed that we would "practice" living together.

"What?" shrieked her friends. "*Practice* living together? That's like 'practicing' being pregnant—you either are or you aren't. You have to commit. What did you just knit him, a vest? There you have it. No sleeves. Only half a commitment."

My more skittish friends lifted their eyebrows, too. "Don't make the mistake of accepting a sweater," they advised. "If you don't have sleeves, you've still got a chance. But once you get fitted for those sleeves . . ."

But, before the next winter—our second together—she selected naturally colored Dorset rustic yarn and a classic Penny Straker pattern, and made a vest with sleeves. That is, a full-length sweater. And our "practice" has evolved, too. We're trying to work out a full pattern for a life together—from a scarf to a vest to a design that includes the sleeves my friends were so wary of. Not to worry, I tell them. I like the fit.

The Sweater
Charmian Christie

I knew we were in trouble when the cuff tore.

Kevin had snagged it on a door, or while he'd been doing yard work or fixing the car. He wasn't sure. It might have happened that day or a week ago.

"Can't you fix it?" he asked.

"Sure," I said. "Should be easy enough." That night, I unraveled the cuff, slipped my needle through stitches standing at attention, and reknit my work. When I cast off, I ran my fingers along the smooth, fresh edge and smiled. Good as new.

The Sweater had begun as a desperately romantic idea for a first-Christmas-together present. With only ten days to make the perfect gift, I scoured shops for rich umber brown wool to match his hair. When I found the color, I raced home and designed a warm, sporty sweater for my exciting new boyfriend.

Each night, I sat in bed, watching the only TV channel I could get in my student flat and knitting until four in the morning. Late-night TV numbed my mind, but it couldn't dull the ache in my cramped fingers. I worked for hours without a break. I questioned my sanity. But gradually, The Sweater inched into life.

Christmas morning, I knit while my family opened presents. I set the needles aside long enough to unwrap my gifts and snatched them up instantly again after giving the donor a hasty thank-you hug. Midafternoon, I cast off the last stitch and darned in the loose threads. Like a mother swaddling her newborn, I wrapped The Sweater in tissue paper and tucked it into its box.

When Kevin opened his gift, he shook The Sweater out, scattering the tissue and ribbons. He grabbed the collar, holding it close to his face, and probed for the nonexistent tag. "You made this?" he demanded.

"Yes," I whispered, afraid he wouldn't like it.

"No one's ever made me a sweater before," he said, yanking

The Sweater over his head. "I love it!" The wool muffled his words, but I could feel his smile.

I was so relieved I nearly cried.

Kevin wore The Sweater every time I saw him for the next month. He refused to take it off. He even slept in it, he told me. How sweet, I thought.

I was less impressed when he wore it to drywall his basement.

"You'll ruin it," I told him as he lifted a panel of Sheetrock into place.

He shrugged and drove a screw into a stud. I left the room, unable to watch, second thoughts whirling about me like drywall dust.

When he finally emerged from the basement, he looked like a gingerbread man coated in icing sugar. He brushed the powder from his clothes, but The Sweater remained ashen and gritty. I slapped his arm, and a cloud of dust leapt from the sleeve.

"No problem," he said. "I'll just throw it in the wash."

"It's pure wool." I envisioned a child-sized sweater being pulled from the dryer. "I'll hand-wash it."

The rinse water resembled liquid cement. As I gently squeezed the soggy wool, I suspected his love for me was as careless and nearsighted as his treatment of The Sweater. On the ninth rinse, the water ran clear, but chalky silt lined the sink. The fallout, I thought.

We stayed together, but I couldn't always wash away the damage. One day, he handed me The Sweater with a hole gaping in its middle.

"Can't you fix it?"

"I'll try."

As I darned, I knew how a surgeon must feel stitching up an injured daredevil. Eager to save The Sweater, I resented fixing such a preventable injury. The patch disfigured the once-perfect form like an appendix scar.

Within a year, The Sweater was as flecked and mottled as camouflage fatigues. And, soon, the elbows began to complain. Time and negligence were eroding the once-proud stitches. More and more, my sympathies lay with The Sweater, not with the guy who wore it.

Initially, his shirt peered through the disintegrating weave. Eventually, the elbow dissolved.

"Can't you patch it?" he asked, twisting the sleeve to examine the hole.

"No, it's too big," I told him. "I'll have to tear out the sleeve and start again." Fortunately, I had enough wool left to reknit the sleeve.

As I unraveled my work, dust flew from the yarn. He had been working in it again. Seconds dropped away as each stitch released. By the time I had undone the sleeve to the bicep, a couple of hours' knitting lay puddled at my feet in a brownish gray mass.

As I reknit the sleeve, I remembered how different I had felt when I first made The Sweater. Each stitch had encircled the needle in a tiny hug, bringing me closer to him. Anticipation of the new, warm relationship had grown with every row. Now, I whipped the wool around the needle in resentment and frustration, pulling it tight like a noose.

The new sleeve was thicker and darker than its mate, a before-and-after shot of our relationship. The rich brown arm contrasted with the tenuous, graying body. I held The Sweater up to the light. I had created a patchwork Frankenstein.

Only an egg-sized ball of wool remained.

We mutually ignored the numerous small snags that followed. Until the shoulder tore. He had hoisted something heavy—drywall, no doubt.

"Can't you fix it?"

"Not enough wool left."

"Can't you buy more?"

"Discontinued."

The last little ball of brown wool cowered in my knitting basket. When I plucked it from its hiding spot, a limp strand brushed my hand like a failed caress. I unraveled the ball, measuring the yarn between my outstretched arms. As reduced as my patience, it barely spanned from left hand to right. I crumpled the wool into a tangled mass, and lobbed it toward the wastebasket. It landed with a wooly whimper. Only a frayed end drooped over the rim, waving good-bye.

Some Things Just Go On and On
Abha Iyengar

It's a hot-red tomato sweater of thick wool. It hangs heavy and loose on whoever wears it, with a wide boat neck and looong sleeves. It's big, even on a well-built 5-foot-10 man like my husband, for whom it was made.

It was October 1991, and the nip in the air heralded the coming of winter. My soul was full of winter as well, since I felt quite useless watching my four-year-old daughter play in the park. I delighted in her play but felt frustrated about my time. I am a type A personality, with the type's restlessness and constant need to achieve. I did not cherish the hours spent idly and felt terribly tied down. I could not even read while my daughter played, since I had to keep a watchful eye on her.

I hit upon knitting, then, as something I could do while I sat on the park bench. I'd knit a big warm sweater for my husband. I decided on the color there and then. Red spells warmth and brightness and cheerfulness, and I felt I needed a lot of that.

I'd learned to knit as a kid and loved it. I loved the feel of the wool. The kind of yarn, soft or rough, thick or thin, pastel or bright or multihued, did not matter. Yarn felt wholesome and natural and warm. I loved simple ribs, moss stitch, cables. Knitting for me was an art form that produced something useful. Over the years, I had become so good that I could spend hours knitting as I watched television or a movie.

But I had not knit for a long time; the kids kept me busy and it seemed so much simpler to buy a sweater off the shelf. And buying "knit to fit" meant none of my usual trials and errors. I can knit, all right; I can knit any complicated design with enthusiasm and gusto. For scarves, this is fine. Sweaters, on the other hand, need to be shaped; the pieces have to be the right length. And this is where I run into trouble. I have tried to knit from magazines and books, but somehow the item just doesn't come out the way it should.

In the past, making a sweater had required much deliberation and consultation with aunts, my mother, neighbors, anyone else even remotely interested. If the person for whom the item was being knit was present, he or she became a sitting duck, draped with sweater-in-process. Much banter, laughter, and talk went into this process. My family knit our relationships with each other this way. We went through endless cups of coffee, savored the winter sun, exchanged recipes, and sorted out everyday problems along with the strands of wool.

Now that I was married, my immediate family was not on hand to give much-needed support and advice. But I was a big girl now, I thought: Surely I could *knit a sweater* by myself, for heaven's sake! And so it came into being, my first individual attempt at making a sweater from A to Z without any advice from others. It moved fast, since I used bright, thick, washable wool and fat knitting needles. I like to see a sweater grow quickly; the ones made of fine wool and knit with thin needles are soft and pretty, but move at a snail's pace. I have knit them as well, but they try my patience.

My husband loves everything that I cook, make, knit, stitch, and buy for him. He is one of the most undemanding men I know. It could be, of course, that he knows which side his bread is buttered on, as he says with a wry grin. So, though the red sweater was very wide at the neck and loose enough to wear numerous layers of clothing underneath, and the sleeves hung down to cover his hands, he wore it. Cheerfully, too. The '90s was not an age when such sweaters were fashionable, but he didn't mind. My love was woven through every knit and purl, and it felt good to him. As he padded around the house in his pajamas and the red sweater, his spectacles balanced precariously on his nose, he looked like the bear in *Jungle Book* who tells Mowgli to "hang loose."

Later the same year, in Germany for a conference, I fell so ill that I went into a coma. There was little hope of recovery. My husband left work and family and came to be by my side.

With him, to fight the Berlin cold and his helplessness, he brought the red sweater. He stood out among the gray and brown European suits and jackets, the red sweater and his red earmuffs gleaming like beacons of warmth and comfort. His bright, cheerful demeanor made an instant hit with the very humane and capable doctors and nurses. Somehow, they all conspired to snatch me from the jaws of death. My husband brought me home from Berlin alive, wrapped warm in his arms. I still remember the rough, comforting feel of the red wool against my cheek.

For ten years and more, we forgot about the sweater. It lay folded along with other unused clothes. I was loath to give it away, even though it occupied a lot of space. This last January, my seventeen-year-old-son was going with friends to Rajasthan for his architectural studies. Somehow, he came across this sweater and adopted it. It looks so good on him! My happiness (and surprise) knew no bounds when he decided to take it along with him.

The sweater is back in circulation and much in demand. Even his girlfriends took turns wearing it during the trip. I have received a deluge of requests to knit them one, too. Born of frustration, created with love, worn with delight, used as a savior of sorts, and now wrapping another happy generation—yes, some things really do go on and on.

Hang in there, my beautiful tomato red.

My Wife Is a *Knitter*: A Triptych

Jef Buehler

One: Knitting Nirvana

My wife is a *Knitter*. Many are those who knit, but few are the *Knitters*. (If you are reading this now, you are probably a *Knitter* as well.) Anyone can knit and purl enough to make knitted items, but for some, knitting is a state of *being*. My wife is to knitting as Gandhi was to pacifism. Gandhi did not just do peaceful things, he embodied pacifism. He was a pacifist as a state of being. *Knitters* embody knitting.

People are born to be *Knitters*. Or not. While almost everyone (even those who, like me, are dexterity-challenged) can—given enough time, yarn, and patience—learn how to knit, one cannot choose to be a *Knitter*. You either are one or you aren't.

As a student of yoga, I find that *Knitters* are perhaps more yogic than many erstwhile gurus. *Knitters* are the ultimate practitioners of nonattachment, even though, at first glance, it seems to be quite the opposite.

Knitters often are seen hoarding skeins of yarn, just as squirrels lay by acorns for the coming winter. Watching my wife in this seemingly prehibernation mode, her studio looking ever more like a knitting store with yarns spilling out from under her large work table, I used to wonder if and when the end of this *Knitter*'s "winter" would ever come. Yet I have learned over time that this is not collecting for collecting's sake. Nor is this yarn meant to be a personal cache, destined to grow until her last day, then to be taken into the afterlife like treasures in a pharaoh's tomb. Quite the contrary: I have learned that knitting is more about letting go than keeping.

First, there is the obvious practice of nonattachment: *Knitters*, on balance, give away many of the items they create: booties to brothers' babies, sweaters to shelters, hats to husbands, blankets to best friends. *Knitters* create and then release their woolen progeny into the lives of many. This practice often requires serious deliberation, since they are allowing a piece of their soul to leave, perhaps forever. This beautiful practice of giving up speaks to the yogic tradition of *aparigraha* (nonhoarding) as clearly as any act one could perform on the meditation cushion. *Knitters* practice a form of meditative *japa* (recitation), counting stitches, leaving the rest of the world just to *be* while they focus on that which they are creating—another form of letting go.

Even more astounding to the outside observer, particularly if the person comes from a Western cultural tradition, is the nonattachment that *Knitters* show when a piece goes wrong. Several years ago, my wife was knitting the front of a beautiful sweater. One evening, after a few days of working on the piece, she was two-thirds done, on the home stretch, when suddenly she stopped. She had realized that there was a counting error near the beginning of her work. This was not a one-time fluke that she could fix by adding a stitch or some such quick fix. Instead, she ruthlessly slipped the work from her needles and row by row unraveled it, erasing hours of work in a few minutes. The same hands that had toiled to build this sweater now respectfully (if not without a hint of melancholy) pulled out hundreds of knits and purls: *tinK, tinK, tinK, tinK,*

tinK, lurP, tinK, lurP, lurP, tinK, tinK . . . the stitches went as they returned to pure (if curlier) yarn form again.

I have seen only a few of the many times she has done this in her more than three decades of knitting. It is truly an act of letting go. I found it hard as a non-*Knitter* to watch such blatant nonattachment, particularly in my pre-yoga days. In fact, I found myself asking her, "How can you do that?" and "Isn't there another way?"—being attached to the unfolding results of her work more than she was. But creating something precious and unique, expressing love through the skill of our hands over hours and days, and then giving it up to the universe and beginning anew . . . that is a *Knitter*'s way to Nirvana.

Two: International Knitting

My wife is a *Knitter*. She is Swiss and therefore a natural "picker" as compared to a "thrower." There is something intriguing about the basic knitting technique and what that says about a person and their culture. While she has lived here in the United States for almost ten years now and certainly is able to adeptly knit and teach "throwing," she is, at her core, a Continental European.

Think of how most *Amis* (Americans, as the German-speaking Swiss call us) knit: You take a needle and you insert it into a stitch, throw yarn around the needle, bring the needle back through the stitch you first inserted the needle through, finally taking the worked stitch off the needle. This is kind of an indirect approach and has a step more than the "picking" method. Europeans, in contrast, hold the yarn behind the work and pick up loops with a single, precise movement. We Americans loop around back and over, eventually arriving at our destination, and then meander back again; they get right to the point.

We Americans regularly express ourselves this way, too: A little bob, a little weave, and we back into expressing our points, ideas, and feelings. We rarely just clearly state things, like: "OK, this is it!", "I think it makes you look fat," or "I like having 372 leftover skeins of yarn around the house. Deal with it!" Europeans tend to be more direct (some may say blunt) in their approach to self-expression. Picking is more efficient and potentially faster because it requires fewer movements than throwing. It gets (as it were) right to the point.

Being in a thrower-picker marriage comes with challenges. I am very much of the American indirect "thrower" culture, and this creates—shall we call them *challenges?*—in communicating with my "picker" wife. Pickers can come across as being picky and picking on you, while thrower-folk throw words around (and around) and in the end may not have said much. Or perhaps more, or less, than they intended.

Neither picking nor throwing, in communication or knitting, is better than the other method. Sometimes one approach flows better for a certain project or in a given situation, mood, and relationship. What really matters is that we appreciate each other's knitting efforts, regardless of how the hands that made them *made* them, and that we accept each other, as woven tapestries of experiences, culture, and personality, in that same way.

Three: Word Knitting

My *wife is a* Knitter.
She knits love—
spilling her heart
out into woven form

from her hands and fingers,
creating warmth
that envelops,
hugs,
and holds
me (and others)
with care . . .
Using mathematics
that would beguile most scientists,
from her mind's eye
she meditatively births
something   often beyond adjectives—
that had never existed before,
bringing it into the realm of the world
one knit, one purl
at a time.
My *wife is a* Knitter.

The Bind-Off: A Knitting Mystery
Stephen D. Rogers

Dave entered my sewing room with a hangdog expression, closing the door behind him gently.

I smiled, my needles flashing. "What's up?"

My husband cleared his throat. "I know this is my night to watch the kids, but there's been a murder."

"Did you explain to the chief that I'm knitting?"

"I tried. He still wants me to take over the investigation since I'm the senior homicide detective."

"The children are sure to get in the way: touching the evidence, bothering the witnesses, waving at the police photographer. You know how they are."

Dave nodded, taking a deep breath. "I was hoping you could—just this once—trade nights. I'll skip my card game and you can knit tomorrow."

I nearly lost my rhythm. Not knit? My husband must have been bucking for another promotion so he could afford to buy me that set of jade needles with the gold inlays and the platinum tips. But I held my tongue, saying instead, "Tell me about this murder of yours."

Dave leaned back against the bookcase where I stored my skeins, sorted by material, color, and weight. "Someone killed Pat Tern, the woman who runs the Crafts Corner."

"How awful."

"Suffocated her with yarn, if you can believe it."

I shook my head. "What a terrible waste. I hope at least it was only a cheap synthetic. Of course Pat would probably rather have been killed with a hand-painted cashmere."

"I don't think they mentioned the material when they called me." Dave pulled a notebook from his pocket. "No. 'Clumps of black and white yarn.'"

"Any suspects?"

"Three. Pat taught knitting classes and apparently would track down and seduce the husband of any student who started to surpass her skill. Three women from the current workshops fit that description."

"Names?"

Dave glanced down at his notebook again. "Rebecca

Smith. Crystal Carver. Lita Hummelbach. All of them claim to be innocent, but none has an alibi for the time of the murder."

"And you have no witnesses."

My husband shrugged. "No witnesses and no useful physical evidence. The detective working the case has come up empty." Dave paused. "The chief is hoping I'll see something that everybody else missed."

"Murder should never go unpunished."

"No."

I could tell Dave was waiting for me to agree to his plan.

"Well, whatever her personal faults, Pat ran a good shop and she'll be sorely missed. Crystal."

"Crystal?"

"Pick her up. Rather, have someone else pick up Crystal. She's your murderer."

Dave stepped forward. "How do you know?"

"She's an artist who wanted to sign her work. You said Pat was suffocated by a mixture of black and white yarns. Contrasting colors. CC. Crystal Carver. She's the one who killed Pat Tern."

"I'll go call it in." My husband started toward the door.

"Dave?"

"Yes?" He paused, one hand on the knob.

"You might want to give them baths before you put the children to bed. Just a suggestion."

Real Men Knit
Dawn Goldsmith

A knitted square featuring a diamond pattern lies on the desk next to my computer. It serves to restore my creativity and acts as a reminder.

I grew up in a culture that defined specific roles for men and women. As as a pampered only daughter, I acquired my knowledge mainly from books, whether about philosophy or bed making. When I married, I couldn't fry an egg without a recipe. I required the proper tools before I could start any project.

My husband, a brawny linebacker in high school and a muscular factory worker when I married him in 1971, approached life from a different angle. He did what interested him and learned best by trial and error.

I hated errors.

Derrol hunted rabbits and squirrels. He fished in winter as well as summer, and he rushed into every contact sport that required a ball and strategy.

He knew how to build a tree house. He knew how to dribble gas into the carburetor, pop the clutch, and get his cranky little Renault running again.

His mom recruited him, the oldest of six kids, at a young age to help with domestic chores. He could whip up a batch of macaroni and cheese while saving his sister's doll from his hatchet-wielding brother. His mother sewed most of her children's clothing, and he was familiar with patterns and fabric. He could baste a hem. He had even stitched some crewel embroidery.

I dreamed of being "the little wife." I'd bake bread, keep an immaculate house, take care of my man while adhering to the feminist ideal of working outside the home. We quickly determined that Derrol could cook better and clean more efficiently than I. He taught me to keep house.

It wasn't until a year into our marriage that I realized what a Renaissance man he was, and is.

We relished our time together. In the evenings we sat side-by-side on the couch watching television or listening to music. I'd pick up my knitting—one of the few needle crafts his mother didn't do. He watched and questioned. "How do you cast on stitches? What are the differences in the stitches?"

I showed him my knitting book and demonstrated what little I knew, which was basically how to cast on, how to knit and purl, and how to tie off the finished piece. He practiced. When he discovered a dropped stitch and unraveled what he'd made, I figured that was the end of it.

Two weeks later, though, I found a pot holder in his lunch box. "What's this?" I asked, waving the off-white square in the air.

He looked up. "Oh, just something I made at work."

I examined it more closely.

The 6-inch, perfectly knit square boasted a delightful geometric pattern beginning with a knit center diamond. A stockinette border came next, surrounded by a knit border. The borders alternated until the square ended in plain knit stitches.

"You made this?" I asked. "What did you use for yarn? For

needles? Where did you get the pattern?" I couldn't believe he'd sat at work among his traditional macho brethren, knitting.

He shrugged, more interested in finding a snack than discussing the pot holder. But he took it out of my hand and looked at it. "I found a cone of string at work, and that's what I used for yarn."

"But the needles," I said. "What did you knit it with?"

He laughed. "Well, they don't have any knitting needles lying around in rubber factories. But I found a couple of bolts, 8 inches long. I filed them to a point, then cast on stitches. It took a while to get the pattern worked out. I ripped it out a lot."

"But what about . . . ?" I hesitated.

He waited for me to finish.

"What about the guys?" I said. "Didn't they tease you?"

He grinned. "Tease me? Nah. Once they saw what I was doing, they wanted me to make some for their wives."

Now when I turn from the computer and pick up that pot holder, I think of the patient man who knitted it. As I touch each stitch, I remember the lessons he has taught me about carburetors, jitterbug fishing lures, and Hail Mary football passes.

Somewhere between the cooking, cleaning, and tire-changing sessions, he taught me about rules, gender roles, and when to ignore them.

Not Fair!

Christine Basham

I always wanted to knit, to crochet, to make my own lace. It all sounded so feminine and lovely and high-minded. If I could just master these simple arts, I'd be a Real Woman.

Somehow, though, whatever I tried didn't work out.

Pregnant with our first baby, and surrounded by a group of friends who carried yarn wherever they went, I thought, "This is the natural time to get crackin'." I asked Sara to give me a lesson or two, just to get started.

Watching me knit, she laughed so hard her eyes watered. Rarely do I have the opportunity to bring anyone such joy.

"C'mon, Christine, this is supposed to be relaxing," she said. "You look like the needles are trying to kill you. Don't fight; knit."

That Zen-like tranquillity of a knitting woman? Not for me. My hands cramped, my face throbbed with tension. Could I do it? Not miss a stitch? Not make a mistake? At the end of each session, Sara would shake her head and pull out my stitches.

"I'll buy you a set of fatter needles, Christine. You're too tense."

The fatter needles/smoother yarn/cheaper materials/ higher-quality materials/better instruction booklet/samples from Sara's home piled up, but none of them made much difference. No matter how long I worked at it, I was still incapable of knitting an attractive article of clothing. In fact, I could hardly knit at all. My fingers wrapped themselves around the needles with a force the envy of any hit man wielding a garrote. I chewed the lipstick off my lips, drew blood, cursed.

"I give up. I don't care what anyone says, knitting is *not* easy. I can't do it."

Sympathetic friends tried to help. One by one, they watched, gave me tips, but finally gave in. Sara knit my baby a sweet pillow shaped like a strawberry. Kim brought a receiving blanket, complete with a floppy-eared, puppy-faced hood. Jen made a sweater with my son's name across the front. Beautiful things, all of them. The kinds of things I would have made myself, if only I could have.

I surrounded my tiny baby with these warm, fluffy offerings of love, the work of my friends' hands, if not my own. Eventually, I stopped feeling stupid and clumsy and "too tense for those needles." I told myself it was a fluke. Just because these three women could knit and I couldn't didn't make me an incompetent mom. Knitting was just really hard. You had to have a knack for it. You had to learn it as a kid. You had to be superfeminine and patient and naturally one with the yarn.

I trashed my aborted patches of lumpy, holey, pathetic knitting, and left the yarn and the needles and the knitting magazines in a bag in the closet. And, I ignored them—until the day my husband needed a piece of string. I pulled out the yarn, cut him off a length, and left the bag on the couch while I went to the store.

When I came home, my husband was sitting on the couch, flipping through a knitting magazine. "I didn't know you could knit, sweetie," he said. "Why don't you make me a sweater? I'd like that."

I explained to him that knitting was hard. I couldn't do it. I didn't have the background, the training, the temperament, the knack. I was not a Chosen One.

"Maybe we could learn together," he said. I picked up my fat needles, and handed him a normal pair. We cast off together, and I was lost—lost in a world where tongue-chomping and muttered curses mark a truly feminine woman. After an hour or so, my brain overflowing with frustration and disgust, I threw down my needles and looked up at my husband. There he sat, eyes on C-SPAN, and a perfect, even, beautiful patch of knitting flowing effortlessly from his fingertips. His first attempt, and I would gladly have worn anything he created. And he was catching up with the news, too.

Somebody's got to teach that man to play fair.

Side by Each: Friends, Sibs, Colleagues

Three Little Kittens Summa Cum Laude

Nancy Clark

As the students filed into the brightly lit lecture hall, I was struck by how many books each of them was carrying. They all looked to be soberly, seriously in love with literature.

I should have been thrilled. I wasn't. I was terrified.

"I'm only a teaching assistant," I thought as I watched the front row fill up. "Here these kids are, paying a fortune, expecting to sit at the feet of a scholar with a Ph.D. from Oxford or Harvard, and all I've got is a B.A. with a master's in the making, if I can stomach it."

There was the usual foot shuffling and some muted coughing as the class—good old American Lit 101—settled down.

When the silence was almost complete, I cleared my throat and began what sounded to my own ears to be a very poor rendition of Marilyn Monroe chitchatting about Hawthorne, Melville, and Edith Wharton.

"I'm going to pass out the syllabus," I announced and went to the corner of the stage to trot down the steps. I was almost to the third row, when I spotted them: three girls, almost identically dressed in white blouses, blue skirts, and chunky black shoes. Each had a sweater of a different color thrown about her neck: one red, one purple, and one a buttery yellow that instantly made me think of happy summer days on a beach.

As I bent over to hand them the sheets, I noticed something so shocking, I actually stepped back to get a better look. They had knitting bags on their laps!

"Ladies," I said in a pompous voice that made me wonder if I could get a job as a ventriloquist when I flunked out of grad school, "surely you're not planning to knit during the lecture?"

Six innocent, round eyes looked at me. It was like being confronted with a basketful of kittens. Kittens armed with steel needles.

"We tape the lectures," one of them, a stunning redhead, said to me and held up a tiny recorder.

"Ah," I said, thinking that was a more professorial syllable than "Oh."

"We did it all through high school," the brunette said.

"We got straight As," the other brunette said.

"I see." My mind raced through possible scenarios of banishment and discarded them all. If they weren't taking notes, did it count that they were taping my every word? Obviously the answer was yes. I was stymied. "Well, this isn't high school, ladies." With that feeble riposte, I continued up the stairs.

As the days went by, I found my eyes homing in on the trio. Privately I called them the Weird Sisters. Like three harbingers of fate, the three girls spent their time knitting industriously, benign smiles on their faces. Every once in a while, one of them would extend the length of the loose yarn and I'd see the flash of a needle's point like the tip of a sword.

At night, I'd agonize about what I was doing. If they had been male, would I have let them toss footballs around? "Hardly an apt comparison," my psyche would sneer. I thought long and hard about an equivocal manly pursuit. Decoy carving? "Why not?" I asked my psyche, who promptly sneered, "Sawdust, genius."

Just before the November break, I went down the aisle passing out a list of possible topics for the term paper. "That's just lovely," I found myself blurting out.

"Thank you," the redhead said, holding up the most gorgeous sweater I had ever seen, done in nubbly crayon colors. "It's going to be a Christmas present for my mom."

"Lucky woman," I said and looked over at the other two. Brunette number one was hard at work on a pastel baby blanket. Brunette number two was producing some kind of ski hat. With a private sigh, I wondered how fair I had been to these three women by allowing them to indulge in the most domestic of pursuits while surrounded by the nuances of intellectual composition.

I found my fancy straying away from thinking of them as "the Weird Sisters," digging into mythology to come up with better monikers. The redhead turned into Penelope, unraveling her work at night. One brunette was obviously Arachne—

never mind that it was knitting, not weaving; yarn is yarn. Mythological resources exhausted, I called the other brunette Rapunzel. It was the best I could come up with.

When the first term papers came in, I went through the stack immediately. "The Prejudice Against the Independent Woman in Puritan New England" was Arachne's title. A quick thumb-through told me everything I needed to know. Not only had she absorbed all the interpretation I had tossed out to my class like buckets of chub to hungry whale calves, but she had produced an impeccable manuscript of sound argument and reason.

Her two fellow needlewomen had produced equally impressive papers. I had to give all three the As they well deserved and had predicted. But underneath it all, I still wondered about how much they had really, truly grasped. After all, they had looked so sublimely female sitting there with their tapestry bags and their skeins of fluffy color and their flashing needles.

When the term ended, I found a beautifully wrapped parcel on my desk in the lowly basement quarters where teaching assistants lurked. Inside was a funky pair of mohair mittens with cuffs of glittery black wool as vibrant and sparkling as the best prose. Beneath the mittens, the three scholars had enclosed a note: "Thank you for letting us be ourselves."

"You three are the perfect candidates to knit up the world's ravell'd sleeve of care," I said in my thank-you note. "I'm looking forward to learning from you in Shakespeare 202."

Grimace and Old Blue
Jenny Feldon

Little sister,

Progress on Old Blue has resumed. When it got really hot, I had a hard time knitting a sweater, but now the weather is cooler and I've started again. Did you finish Grimace yet? Don't worry about the holes; you can always sew googly eyes over them and make it into a Halloween costume! Say hi to everyone for me—I've got to get back to work in the engine room.

Bah Bah,
Jess

That's an e-mail from my brother Jess, a second-class midshipman in the United States Merchant Marine Academy at Kings Point. Now aboard a U.S. Navy ship delivering supplies to the Persian Gulf, he may be the first cadet to carry blue worsted-weight yarn and size 7 circular needles among his few belongings.

I'm actually four years older; the "little sister" refers to my height. For the longest time, my younger sibling was nick-named "Shrimp Boy" and "Short Stuff"—that is, until he grew 6 inches the summer before his junior year in high school. Now, at 6 foot 3, he towers over me (and never lets me forget it)!

It started last November, when Jess arrived home on a rare

break from the academy, where he's pursuing a bachelor's degree in marine engineering, a commission in the U.S. Naval Reserve, and a third-assistant-engineer's license. He burst into the family room, still clad in his gold-buttoned, double-breasted uniform. I was sitting on the floor, tears of frustration brimming onto my cheeks, negotiating out loud with the giant mass of purple yarn in my lap.

"What are you doing?" Jess asked, incredulous.

"I'm knitting a sweater," I grunted.

"Doesn't look like you're knitting. Where are your needles? It looks more like you're making a mess."

A brief scuffle ensued, but after I surrendered to threats of tickle torture, Jess became serious and eyed my tangled first project with interest.

"I've always wanted to learn to knit," he said. "Let me try."

"What do you mean? Knitting isn't for guys."

"Sure it is. I always thought it would be cool to knit during downtime—you know, during study hall or on the train. Come on, show me how."

Though I'd been a knitter for a mere three days, I did my best to show him the knit and purl stitches. Jess brandished the needles like weapons, gripping them in each fist with ferocious effort. His first few rows of stitches were so tight we had to cut them off the needles with scissors.

"I like this," Jess announced. It was almost midnight; we'd been alternately stitching and swearing for almost three hours without realizing it. "I'm going to knit a sweater while I'm away at sea."

"How can you do that? You don't know how."

"I have a whole week before I leave. I can learn before I go."

He would, too. I knew it. Jess made his first stock purchase in sixth grade, took swing-dancing lessons in high school just for fun, and ran 12 miles every morning at 4 A.M. Whatever he put his mind to was as good as done. Admiring both his ambition and the ease with which he was fielding my jokes about his masculinity, I offered to buy him the yarn and materials he'd need, as an early gift for the holidays.

We arrived early the next day at our local yarn store, Putting on the Knitz, where I'd been taking lessons.

"This is my brother Jess," I told the owners, Don and Janet, who painstakingly teach dozens of neophyte knitters in their tiny, welcoming shop every day from morning to night. "He wants to learn how to knit a sweater, but he's leaving on a ship with the navy next week."

Don looked him carefully up and down, a gleam in his eye at the prospect of having a male pupil—even if only for a week.

"We can do it," Don proclaimed, grinning. He scurried around the small store, grabbing patterns and yarn samples. "Sit here," he told Jess, pointing to an empty folding chair. "We'll start right now."

We spent the next few days sitting around the store's round table, knitting one good stitch for every five mistakes. Jess and I worked diligently on our respective sweaters, looking up occasionally to ask a question or yell for help. Soon, my mass of tangled purple wool was looking remarkably like knit fabric.

"Look," I said to Jess, who was practicing decreases on some extra yarn. "It looks like a purple cone." I handed him the sweater's slightly oblong back.

His blue eyes flashed with mischief. "Actually, Jenny, it looks like Grimace."

Insulted, I grabbed the sweater back, losing a few stitches in the process.

"It does *not!*"

"Does." Jess smirked.

I looked at it carefully, turning it back and forth between my hands, which ached with the unfamiliar, repetitive motions of the craft. It did sort of look like Grimace, the good-natured, pear-shaped creature who appears on the sides of Happy Meal boxes.

"Fine," I admitted. "We can call it Grimace. But if mine has a name, yours has to, too."

After much deliberation, we decided on Old Blue, mostly due to the rich color of the navy yarn Jess had chosen, but also because of the traditional look of the crewneck pattern he was following. The pattern reminded me of old-time sailors and sepia-toned portraits of great-grandparents we'd never met. It was perfect for Jess, whose dedication and stoicism had always seemed reminiscent of an earlier era.

A few days later, Jess carefully packed eight skeins of yarn and the rest of his sweater supplies, along with his uniforms, schoolbooks, and other essentials for his sea voyage, into a giant khaki duffle bag. I hugged him good-bye at the train station, struggling to remain cheerful so he wouldn't see how painful it was for me to watch him go.

Every time he left was difficult for my family, but this time was different. This time, he was headed to a place of conflict and turmoil, and the danger of his mission couldn't be denied. All the things I wanted to tell him swirled around in my mind: *Don't go. Please be careful. Please come home.* But I knew I couldn't say what I was really feeling. I had to be as brave as he was.

"Keep working on Grimace," Jess whispered.

"You keep working on Blue," I whispered back.

He raised his hand in mock salute and hoisted his bag over his shoulder, the knitting needles peeking out from a side pocket. Then he turned and followed a stream of travelers toward the boarding train.

In the days and weeks that followed, I worked on Grimace and slowly improved my knitting skills. At the same time, I felt a connection to Jess, who, all those miles away in foreign waters and beyond communication, was doing exactly the same thing.

When he comes home, I'll have a lot to tell him. I'll be wearing my purple, slightly misshapen, but finished sweater. And he'd better be wearing Old Blue.

Aunt Shirley's Snow Families

Jean Stone

It began at Nimble Thimbles, the church ladies' group that gathered once a week to share time and sociability under the worthy guise of crafting homespun articles—pom-pom hats and mittens, skating socks and wooly scarves—for the holiday church fair.

Aunt Shirley specialized in sweaters. Pullovers, cardigans,

or vests, it didn't matter; simple stockinette or cables, plain or Fair Isle, Aunt Shirley knit them all. Her sweaters could be counted on to add a hefty sum to the fundraising efforts. But after years of knitting, Aunt Shirley was bored.

"I'm tired of making sweaters," she announced one Nimble Thimbles day.

Silence fell across the room. After all, it was not acceptable for church ladies to gasp.

"Well," one of them bravely said (it might have been Margaret, Jane, or Flora), "perhaps we could try something new." This was a daring statement. Although it was the 1970s, change did not always come easily for Congregationalist women whose church had been rooted on the same town green since 1700-and-something.

But the church needed a new boiler and the Sunday school needed supplies. So, bonded by a single purpose, the ladies slowly started to collect different crafts ideas from magazines. It wasn't long before the wooly scarves and mittens gave way to fanciful tree ornaments and fashionable tote bags, colorful wall hangings and soft, sweet doll clothes. The group was infused with new enthusiasm.

Then Aunt Shirley met the snowmen.

Each snowman consisted of a 3-inch Styrofoam ball on the bottom and a 2-inch one on top. Each ball was covered by a white knit "coat," and the top one wore a bright green knit scarf and a red, red knit cap. And each snowman had black felt eyes and black felt buttons and a cheery, red felt smile. In later years, Aunt Shirley said it was that smile that had stolen her heart.

She started small: One, then two, then half a dozen snowmen lined the dry sink in her living room. But Aunt Shirley felt something wasn't quite right, and one night she realized what it was.

"The snowmen needed snow ladies," she said. "And snow children."

And so the snow families were created: three per family, three different sizes.

That year at the church fair, Aunt Shirley's snow families sold out quickly. Encouraged by the response, she set out to make the following year even more successful.

Winter, spring, summer, fall—Aunt Shirley knit up a snowstorm. Even Uncle Ralph—a truck-driving union man who smoked Lucky Strikes and built ham radios and worked in the pits of a race-car track, long before race-car driving was a fad—got in on the act by snipping out the black felt eyes and buttons and the cheery, red felt smiles.

The knitting part was simple—no complicated cables or intricate patterns. But each snow person had something far more special: personality. I don't know whether she did, but I like to imagine that Aunt Shirley gave each a name: the Baker family; and the Drakes; and the Muldoons from down the street. No matter what they were or were not called, by the time each December rolled around, the families that lined the dry sink could have filled up the church pews.

Over the years, Aunt Shirley created hundreds, maybe thousands, of snow families. As she got older and arthritis gripped her hands, she reserved making them only as gifts for special friends: the woman who owned the flower shop, the girl who set up bingo at the senior housing social hall. Even toward the end of her life, when Aunt Shirley had become legally blind, each Christmas she made sure her own family of snow people stood atop her television. Her eyesight might be gone, but her memory was clear.

At her funeral not long ago, the minister stood in the pulpit of the church Aunt Shirley had loved so well, and in the eulogy he said, "Shirley Franklin will be remembered for many things." And everyone there knew what he would mention next.

Today, it is my sister who knits clothes and hats and scarves to help create snow people. Her two daughters help as well, by giving them out as gifts. And each Christmas when I take mine from their storage box, I wonder what Aunt Shirley would think if she knew that her single comment at a Nimble Thimbles meeting would keep on spreading joy, two generations later, one red felt smile at a time.

Competitive Knitting

Beth Walker

Day One

I got through the first of a ten-day intensive seminar on literature, a two-hours-plus marathon of staying seated, trying not to twitch. It may be good to have the habit of keeping one's hands busy, but it can also spill into addiction. Sitting there without handwork was killing me.

After I got home, I ripped out the notebook pages with the ugly doodles that I had resorted to and thought longingly of my knitting. Then it hit me: I had once seen knitting in the hands of the faculty member now leading the seminar.

I went through my knitting stash and chose a project to bring with me to the next class: idiot knitting, size 13 huge needles (fat, wrist-sized ones); inexpensive thick acrylic chenille; and a straightforward pattern. I needed to be able to talk, think, and not worry about cables and counting stitches. The project? A scarf in chocolate brown chenille, with a slit for one end of the scarf to pull through.

Day Two

I read through the pattern, tucked it back into my knitting tote, and went into the classroom. I hitched up to the long table, slipped out my needles, and cast on. This was, for me, a typical project: a heavily revised version of an existing pattern. Ever since I got past the childhood phase of furiously concentrating on knit 2–purl 2, I just don't stick to directions. I always have to do *something* to the pattern.

For my version of this pattern, I cast on twenty stitches, and got to it. Class started, the discussion was lively, and I joined in, keeping my knitting under the table as I worked. Although I'm a slow knitter, I managed in that one session to knit the scarf up through the slit. My notebook was safe from ugly doodles. And my addiction to handwork was satisfied.

Day Three

When I walked into class, I saw a classmate knitting, but something that was as different from my chunky scarf as a piece of knitting could be. She had strung speck-sized seed beads onto crochet thread and was expertly using toothpick-sized needles to knit a gorgeous bag, just big enough to hold, oh, a nickel.

I walked over to her, shoving the bulky chenille out of sight. "That's just beautiful!" I said.

She said, her tone brisk and just a touch smug, "Oh, this? I'm just doing this for fun." She held out the perfect tiny baglet for my inspection.

Fun? It would take me a year of sweating and cursing to make that midget bag.

She continued, "I'm taking a break, since I just finished a Kaffe Fassett sweater."

Hoo boy, now she was name dropping. At least I recognized the designer's name, but my classmate was clearly way out of my knitting league. Beads flashed as her fingers flew through another row.

She smiled at me. "So—are you just learning to knit?"

I mumbled something semipolite, then found a seat at the other end of the table, yanked out my big, fat wad of scarf, and hid it under the table. Up to this moment, I had considered knitting a Zen-like, meditative, and slightly odd habit left over from my childhood. It was something I tried to play down, especially in public.

But now, knitting had moved from a private affair to a competition, and I was losing. In spite of my family's occasional ribbing (get it?), I was in no way our Martha of housekeeping and insider trading. I might pursue the domestic arts, but I rarely caught them. I was always shocked when, once in a while, one of my domestic projects actually turned out right.

No; I was the more inventive variant of a knitter interested in seeing what would happen. This was true in more realms than knitting. For a while I cut my own stencils, not of geese and teddy bears (fond as I am of them) but of Celtic knots and Art Nouveau swirls. I don't do projects to excel at them; I do them to experiment, to play. Knitting is playing with designs and patterns, yarn and color.

One look at my classmate's size 000 (or maybe more) needles, and I knew she would never understand. I smoothed the length of chenille, picked up those fat needles, and knit.

Day Ten

On the last day of class, I finished up a second scarf, an ascot from a vintage '40s pattern. I had made two scarves, learned more about literature, and left notebook pages free of desecration.

My classmate had finished the beaded baglet, along with a baby sweater knit on size 2 needles.

Day Eleven

This morning, I found myself thinking more about knitting than about literature. I am glad people like to knit complex patterns on size 2 needles. I wish I liked doing that. But I don't. Instead, I play with yarns and patterns. I don't begin to compete with technical knitters. And maybe that's okay. I opened my knitting bag, looked down at the gold-and-silver ladder yarn of my current project, and laughed. I'll know I'll lose any knitting competition I might inadvertently enter, but it doesn't matter, so long as I can play with yarn and feed my addiction to handwork!

The Live-Lobster Sweater

Suzanne Strempek Shea

I wore black.

This was a no-brainer, since I would be attending a funeral. And I was honestly sad. So the color wasn't just tradition; it was a true mirror of my emotions. My outfit consisted of a black Nehru jacket that a friend had given me after the annual weeding of her closet, a long black skirt I'd bought in an Irish department store upon being invited to attend a theater performance where I ended up sitting in an audience generally attired in pastel track suits, and eight-dollar zip-front boots from Ames's end-of-season clearance rack. For the first time in the three years since I'd sworn off them, I pulled on nylons. Black nylons. I pulled on black nylons because I wanted to look proper. I wanted to look proper because I had loved Zedra. And now she was dead.

I had met Zedra on a Tuesday morning, twenty-three years ago, when she looked across the top of her computer terminal and greeted me. It was my first day of work as a full-time newspaper reporter. Fate could have plunked me down in the ergonomically correct office chair opposite that of the entertainment editor, who regularly threw pieces of office equipment as a stress-reducing measure. Or I could have landed across from the nice but nicotine-addicted copy editor, barely visible through her perpetual cloud of Virginia Slims exhaust. But on that first day, as I did for most of the four years that followed, I sat facing Zedra Jurist Aranow. And one of her handknit sweaters.

I can't recall the exact one she wore that day, but I remember admiring it. Zedra replied that she'd made it, and I told her that I knit, too. Immediately we found the common denominator that would bond us in spite of the age gap between us—Zedra was then a couple of years short of retirement age, while I was a twenty-one-year-old, just forty-eight hours past getting my college diploma. Zedra caught me just as I was making the swing into the realities of adulthood and the bigger world.

She and her husband, Wally, had four adult kids of their own, but that didn't stop her from unofficially adopting others, including most of her co-workers. Gently, wryly, laughingly, she nurtured us, Monday through Friday from 7 A.M. to 3 P.M., in between writing her notes in pencil on scrap newsprint and hunt-and-pecking out lifestyle features and a weekly humor column.

What Zedra's people at the paper had in common was, first, our place of employment, and second, that Zedra had spotted in us something with which she could connect. It might be our creativity, puns, semiprecious gemstones, a particular Chinese takeout joint, preferred color of daylily, or taste in books. In some cases, the connection was more basic: Zedra saw in someone a confusion, loneliness or muddling that she ached to ease.

The luckiest among us had one further thing in common: a Zedra original. At some point, if you were one of "her" people, she'd knit you a sweater—made, perhaps, for a special occasion, or perhaps for no reason at all. She could craft elaborate cables and often tried to lure me from my Norwegian knits into the world of Arans. But the sweaters she most enjoyed creating were what she called "leftovers," crafted from a dazzling palette of stash. A plain field of black or brown or gray would sprout circles of color or stripes of variable widths in a succession you'd initially never think would work. Unless you were Zedra, in which case the resulting cardigan or pullover would be the stuff of boutiques.

Zedra's smarts, her wit, her caution, her wise advice, her recipe for chestnut stuffing—most people got their share when they stopped at her desk, or pulled up a chair in the break room. She told me many things: that our lifestyle department—formerly the "women's section"—was a perfect home for a young writer, being a microcosm (she used that word) of all the subjects you would want to cover. She told me to loop my extra rubber bands on doorknobs so they'd be available in all rooms should they ever be needed. She said that you should never throw out even a few inches of scrap yarn (you never know when you might need just a few stitches of that color). She instructed me to mail gifts with fun packing like candy instead of plain old paper. She told me to get along with less—after all, at my age, she'd owned only two pairs of stockings, one drying in her Murray Hill bathtub, the other on her legs while she was out writing ad copy for Manhattan's Bonwit Teller. She tossed out these bits and pieces across the top of her computer and over to me.

I have a photo of Zedra as I best remember her: from the bridge of her nose on up, that being my view when I looked above my screen most of those four years. Her blue eyes peer at you over her bifocals. Her short white hair is billowy but tidy. I gave her a copy of the picture, and she took it home to hang on her refrigerator, adding a caption: "You are being watched."

It was true: I knew she had her eyes on me, and on my life. She trooped out to the parking lot to check out the Chevette that was my first new-used car, fussed over the pup I got from the SPCA, delivered to the door of my first house—a lake-front A-frame—a counted cross-stitch of a leggy water bird. She quizzed me on my social life, hugged me in the reception line after my wedding ceremony, took me out to our favorite Vietnamese restaurant when I told her I was moving on to another paper.

She was always delighted about something, even though she had health concerns, an aged mother, and a big old house that needed all the tending that big old houses do. Zedra had so many of the regular problems so many of us have, but she focused on the good in her life. In later years, she actually banned me from asking the simple question "How are you?" "There comes a time in life when there are much better things than health to talk about," she informed me in an uncharacteristically terse tone during one of our meetings at a pancake house.

Whenever we met, we always wore our latest knitted creations or brought works in progress for show and tell. If I had nothing new to show, I'd wear my treasured Zedra original. It was a heavily cabled pullover of St. Andrew's yarn in a color called "Live-Lobster"—a deep blacky green with tiny flecks of gem tones. I'd picked the color from a sample card before a co-worker headed to New Brunswick on vacation. She returned with a sack of yarn that, in its skein state, looked disappointingly plain and a lot less rich than the sample had led me to believe. Nonetheless, I gave the skeins to Zedra and left the pattern up to her. After what seemed like no time, I came into work one morning to find on my desk a gorgeous front, back, and two sleeves. Zedra loved knitting. She abhorred finishing. She left to me the sewing and the collar. I liked the fact that the sweater was a collaboration.

Now I was going to her funeral.

In line to sign the mourners' book, I felt a tap on my shoulder. I turned to see a co-worker I'd last set eyes on when I was driving the Chevette. Claudia stood there in a sweater coat dotted with a rainbow of familiar-looking leftoverish colors. Zedra had e-mailed me about helping Claudia get into knitting, and now before me was Claudia, in something she'd made with our friend's guidance. As I chose a seat, I heard my name. The editor of the section for which Zedra and I had written caught my eye. Bold aqua cables—I knew from whose needles they'd come—and dolman sleeves wrapped around me in a wordless hug. A hand reached to shake mine; the sleeve above it was striped black and white and gray, created by the woman we were there to honor, and to whom we would say good-bye.

Zedra's niece did the eulogy. She stood at the podium in a striped soft brown and rust pullover I'd admired as she'd passed earlier. My suspicions were confirmed as she proclaimed it a Zedra original, made of leftovers, with Zedra's trademark intentional error to show that the piece was hand-done. In this sweater's case, the error was a short length of yarn poking from the inside of an upper sleeve. To show that a human had made it, that was Zedra's intention. Thought and skill, the gift of time, work, and love; all that a machine cannot crank out—that was what the bit of yarn spoke to.

After the service, her casket was rolled down the aisle, pale plain wood in the custom of her faith. What followed was anything but plain: Zedra's family, both her family of flesh and her family of the heart, so many of them in radiant Zedra knits. Pullovers, vests, cardigans, a shawl. More stripes. Solids bearing patterns she managed with nary a chart.

And me in my unknit black. Back at home in my stack of sweaters was the Live-Lobster. On a day when I couldn't have put two words together to say how much Zedra had meant to me, that sweater would have said it all.

At home again, I dug into my stack of sweaters, pulled off the Nehru jacket and pulled on my Live-Lobster. Finally I was properly dressed for this day. I sat down at my computer and began to write this story:

I wore black. . . .

The Fort River Knitting Circle

Martie Stothoff

Grade 3, Fort River Elementary School, Amherst, Massachusetts
(with orthographic assistance from Molly Wolf)

This story is for Laural Homstead, my knitting teacher, who started the Fort River Knitting Circle.

It all started when my neighbor Linda knit me a bright red hat. When I saw the hat, I thought, "I wish I could do that." Then at school—it was sometime in the fall—Emma and

Kelli were talking about a knitting club. Talking to them, I realized I could soon make wonderful things like Linda did. Little did I know that it takes a while to get the hang of knitting. I got really frustrated with my knitting, and I kept ripping it out.

Then, before Christmas, I forgot my knitting over at my school. My friend Kelli gave me some blue yarn and needles. So I started to knit again. Then, at Christmas, I started to run out of yarn. But, luckily, I got a brand-new ball of yarn for Christmas! It is multicolored yarn. My knitting teacher, Laural, taught me how to add a new color on. So I added on my new multicolored yarn.

This past year, I've been working on a scarf. I am one of many scarf makers. I know Emma, Olivia, and Cassie are making scarves. Some people are making a purse, like Alanna. And Maya just finished a hat, and it looks great! My next project might be something on the silly side, like Amanda, who is making a head thing.

I've really enjoyed this experience and hope to do it next year. This year, our club got lots of newcomers and I hope they do it next year, too. It's kind of like a little cycle, because Emma and Kelli got me interested. I got Alanna and Brianna interested, who got Victoria interested.

My favorite time to knit is before I go to bed, or when I'm frustrated. My friend Josh sometimes has problems at school. Then my teacher Pam lets him knit so he can relax.

I hope this story has encouraged you to learn to knit.

Knit TWO Together

Jeannine Bakriges

"You'll only have two or three *really* good friends in your life; many nice acquaintances, but only a few true friends . . . that is, if you're lucky." My mother said this (or something like it) years ago. I believe her. Thank goodness, I've been lucky.

Susan and I met more than fourteen years ago. Our husbands both worked at Simon's Rock College in Great Barrington, Massachusetts. My husband had recently been appointed activities director. We and our two sons had just settled into our dormitory apartment at the beginning of the schoolyear when the equally new athletic director arrived with his pregnant wife, Susan. Feeling a bit blue and isolated in our new surroundings, I invited Susan over for a cup of tea. We discovered that we both had art degrees and were from the Midwest. A good common denominator, I thought. But as we talked, the conversation took a new and different turn.

I've been told that when I love something, I should sell stock in it because my enthusiasm bubbles over. And so it was with knitting. I'd learned to knit as a child and rediscovered it when my own older boy was born. I'd only known Susan for an hour, but I couldn't resist showing her my latest project, knitting books, and magazines. Actually, I didn't just show her, I babbled nonstop. It's amazing she didn't turn and run.

Our first visit led to many more as we both eagerly waited the birth of her child. Inevitably (I couldn't help myself!) the talk always veered toward knitting. I kept pulling out more books and magazines. I sometimes wondered whether she was intrigued with the artistic and expressive possibilities of knitting, or whether she was too polite to say she was bored to death. But she kept coming over.

Quite unexpectedly, one day Susan shocked me by asking if I would teach her how to knit. As a devotée of Elizabeth Zimmermann and Meg Swansen, I took the circular needle approach in teaching Susan the fundamentals. Her son Matthew was born by then, and her first project was a little olive-green circular-yoke sweater. Impish green booties followed. Soon we were both knitting the same sweater design, Susan for her Matthew and me for my youngest, Alexander. Jointly we translated the magazine pullover pattern into circular knitting. The needles' clicking bound our friendship closer together.

Months went by and Susan discovered she was ill. Diagnosed with a rare blood disorder that would be fatal if left untreated, she and her family took the advice of doctors and scheduled a bone marrow transplant. One of her sisters was the donor. The operation was successful, but Susan would have to endure months of confinement. She spent the first two months in isolation at the Yale Medical Hospital. By this time, Susan was a confirmed knitter. She wanted to knit while she was hospitalized, but everything she touched had to go through a high-heat sterilization process. This ruled out her favorite fiber, wool. She remembered some cotton yarn in her stash at home and hoped it would survive sterilization. The hospital staff treated the yarn, but the fiber turned so stiff and unyielding it was unknittable. Reluctantly, she had to relegate knitting to dreams of future projects.

Susan spent almost the entire next year confined to home. Anyone visiting her had to wear a mask and surgical gloves. After she had been home for a few weeks, I went to see her. My heart almost stopped at first sight of her. All her hair had fallen out from radiation, and she had lost a great deal of weight. I couldn't believe this was my beautiful friend Susan. At least she was back to knitting, she told me; she had started a wool sweater for a friend.

Twice a week she had to go back to Yale for blood work. Her doctors were alarmed when her red blood cell count dropped dramatically. "What are you doing differently?" they asked. Just knitting again, Susan said, with wool. Now that she thought about it, the wool smelled faintly of mothballs— not something Susan herself used, but perhaps the wool had picked up the smell in the mill or the store where she'd bought it. The doctors did a bit of research and found that the chemicals in mothballs have been linked to leukemia—an eye-opener to her, and to me too. Ever since, we've been particularly careful to avoid moth repellants.

Thankfully the year of confinement ended and Susan and I could meet regularly again. But that time cemented our friendship. It has grown ever since, even though both of our families have left Massachusetts for other states. Fiber festivals and workshops have drawn Susan and me into adventures in New York, Toronto, Maine, Maryland, and other places. We discuss our knitting projects via phone and e-mail.

Over the years, I ventured into the fascinating realm of handspinning and dyeing my own yarns, but Susan stuck adamantly to knitting, saying that she'd best not get involved with any more projects than she already had going. But on one of our autumn trips to our favorite New York Sheep and

Wool Festival, she surprised me yet again; she came home toting a state-of-the-art spinning wheel and an Australian Shepherd mix puppy. Not surprisingly, the yarns she's learned to spin are superb. Her spinning and knitting have won many awards, including the coveted "Best of Show" at the Maryland Sheep and Wool Festival.

On the plane ride home from that trip to Maryland, we started talking about how much fun it would be to go into business together, doing something in the fiber arts we both loved. Before we knew it, we were nearly shouting the possibilities to each other, excitement growing by the minute. "The Copper Moth" began to incubate right then and there. A few months later, she called to say, "We need to start now!" In January 2002, we signed papers making us partners in a Web-based business that features our naturally dyed silks, wools, and other sumptuous fibers for handspinners.

I'd be silly to say this story is over. Our adventure continues, because, after all . . .

Knit 2 tog = friends forever.

Letter to My Sister

Janet Blowney

My older sister is a knitter. I say this proudly and with some degree of amazement, because for many years she was a confirmed, avid "I swear I'll never do this" non-knitter.

Although I was willing, I did not teach her to knit. Friends taught her, and she has learned with great speed and acumen. I'm sorry that I missed her debut, that my hands did not help her shape her first knits, purls, and yarnovers. Younger sisters get few chances to teach their older sisters, and I regret missing this one.

On reflection, however, I see that I can still provide her with essential advice. Her friends set her forth on a precarious path without warning her of the hazards along the way. They neglected to tell her about stash, and so I will.

Dear Karen,

As your first project comes to an end, you'll tuck aside the remaining yarn. Perhaps you'll use it to mend your sweater as it ages, or to make a matching cap. You're a real knitter now, and you have begun to acquire the requisite yarn stash.

Yarn stashes usually start small, but they can spiral rapidly out of control. Soon, you'll buy the yarn for your next project, picking up a few extra hanks on sale. You'll receive wool as gifts. You'll accept the surplus yarns of others. Over time, this yarn will be joined by more of the same, in an insidious process known as stash creep or stash bloat. If stash creep goes unchecked, you and your family may find yourselves eating meals off jumbo-sized Rubbermaid containers filled with yarn. You may even face eviction.

You are among knitters now, and you will hear the myths, lies, and misconceptions about stash. If you believe them and act on them, stash can overrun your life like kudzu and destroy it. If you understand these lies for what they are, your life need not be controlled by your stash. Here are the top five lies about stash.

1. **Yarn gets lonely.** *This is a lie. You do not need to provide your yarn with friends. Nor does yarn call out to other yarn, inviting it into your home without your knowledge or consent. Unattended yarn does not mate in your closets and bureau drawers, resulting in litters of small skeins that take over your household. You, and you alone, are ultimately responsible for the yarn that enters and occupies your home.*

2. **Stash is a home improvement material.** *Not. Disregard those magazines and book covers that show wall units full of yarn, grouped by color and attractively displayed, with an antique basket overflowing with handspun wool as an accent piece. In the average home, yarn displayed in this way is not decoration; it is a supermarket for moths. Likewise, do not listen to those who insulate their homes with yarn or furnish them with beanbag chairs and packing boxes stuffed with wool. The R factor of wool is unimpressive. A tablecloth over a cluster of packing boxes is not a dinner table, and beanbag chairs are just as ugly and uncomfortable now as they were in the 1960s. People telling you otherwise are yarn junkies; they cannot be trusted.*

3. **Stash is a retirement plan.** *You wish. Stash is not a reliable 401(k), IRA, or pension plan. You cannot eat stash, and most landlords, doctors, and pharmacists do not work on the barter system. Put away some money for your old age.*

4. **A large stash saves money.** *This is a myth. Your genetic heritage of good Scot mixed with thrifty Yankee may predispose you to acquire small lots and balls of yarn "too*

good to throw away." This may seem frugal. In fact, because these bits and pieces are insufficient to complete a project, you will be forced to supplement them with fresh purchases, which drain your pocketbook and bloat your stash. And, by the way, driving excess yarn around in the trunk of your car reduces fuel efficiency.

5. **You cannot die until you have used up your stash.** Reality check: Much of your stash will come from the estates of deceased knitters. Your estate planning should include a brutal critique of your own stash, to ensure that you bequeath only the worthiest fibers. Not to put too fine a point on it, but as your younger sister and possible heir, I would welcome kid mohair, qiviut, and cashmere.

Having warned you about the perils of excess stash, let me also encourage you to find joy in the raw materials of our craft. You need not always resist the enticing call of fine cottons, silks, or wools, or the eye-popping palettes and seductive feel of designer yarns. Add to your stash, but do so judiciously. Your yarn should liberate you, not imprison you. When yarn runs through your fingers, worries vanish, replaced by the rich and soothing colors and textures of your stash. A reasonable amount of good yarn is a very real comfort in times of trouble.

But if you find yourself lurking about the copier room at work, waiting to snatch the empty boxes and mentally calculating how many skeins each carton will hold, stop right there. Beware the bloat.

Love,
Your kid sister

Sweaters from "The Keep"

Marge Wooley

More than forty years ago, I spent eight summers of my youth at Hillsboro Camp in Hillsboro, New Hampshire. It was a rich experience. I learned how to get along with fifteen-plus cabin mates, to paddle a canoe in a straight line across the lake, to cook a crumb cake in a reflector oven, to wait patiently for a steak-and-fried-potato dinner after an exhausting climb to the top of Mount Kearsage. And I learned how to knit a one-piece sweater.

Getting along with others has been invaluable. I haven't paddled a canoe for many years, but I still could. I don't eat crumb cake anymore, but it was delicious (except for the unbaked lumps). I'd gladly wait patiently for steak and fried potatoes cooked over the open fire. And I still have my one-piece sweater.

When I was a camp counselor, we had access to a small rustic cabin called The Keep Out, or more commonly just The Keep. Off-limits to all campers, it gave us a chance to skulk off and have a smoke or some much-needed down time.

One cool summer, many of the counselors decided to take up knitting. (The previous year, we'd taken up smoking corncob pipes.) On the advice of our fellow counselors and experienced knitting sisters Sue and Mary, we sent away to a discount yarn shop in Jersey City for our yarn and needles. The yarn finally arrived, and we began our projects with great excitement. The goal was to keep the sweaters as simple and easy as possible. Sue and Mary developed a pattern for us to follow. I chose bulky yarn and huge needles—I'm always in a hurry to finish everything I do.

We started at the back and worked up to the neck. The knitting sisters had us craft a neck hole and then start down the front, making a tuniclike creation. We then picked up stitches on the shoulders and knit in the direction of imaginary wrists. As I recall, the best part of the project was being able to spread the sweater across my lap to warm me as I knit on those chilly August nights in the beautiful hills of New Hampshire. My sweater was done in time to wear it to the year-end banquet. But by that night the weather had changed; it was far too hot to wear my bulky handknit sweater.

After the one-piece sweater, I made a few more things, but I lost the habit of knitting. I have remained very good friends with many of the former campers and counselors, however. About two years ago, a fellow "Hillsboro Girl" urged me to start knitting again; she even supplied me with yarn, needles, and a pattern. I'm back to it and have managed to move on from the one-piece-sweater level to more complicated projects. What matters more, though, are the friendships that Hillsboro Camp knit together. My one-piece sweater doesn't fit me anymore, but the friendships do—and always will.

The Artist

E. B. Clutter

I was drawn to the work right away. I mean, how often does one come across a coat that might have been worn by King Henry VIII? In sheer size, but also in shape and color, it seemed right off an old painting, and so exquisitely made. Right beside it was a smaller coat, different in color and detail yet equally beautiful and grand. Museum pieces! And there were two amazing chain mail helmets that Beowulf might have worn. Fabulous they were, these and the other garments I could see hanging on mannequins in the little Toronto shop.

"Take a look. They're all knitted. This one might fit you," the salesclerk said, leading me to a doublet proper enough for Sir Walter Raleigh. "Look at the sleeve and shoulder details, the slimming peplum," she smiled, fingering the doublet fondly, turning back the collar so I could see the interior finishing. "Fabulous with a slim black skirt and boots, don't you think? Try it on!"

I demurred.

"It is rather expensive," she admitted, replacing the hanger, "but the artist is very talented and very special. And she's generally getting the prices she asks."

"There aren't too many people with learning and talent enough for this," I agreed, wandering from one gorgeous piece to another. I'd had no intention of stepping inside this shop, but now that I was over the threshold, I was mesmerized.

"She's a history buff, but practical, and every piece is wearable," the salesclerk's smooth voice assured me. "Silk lining, good buttons. No problem in dry cleaning. Like a lifetime investment. You'd have it for years."

"Actually, the items look really heavy. I don't think I could ever wear them," I said. It was summer and I was sweating, even in the air-conditioned shop. "But any of them would be absolutely gorgeous on a display stand or hanging on a wall." I stepped up to examine the details of what looked like Peter Pan's hunting jacket. The artist had looped a few of the various fibers through the tag, wools and ribbons in subtle shades of fawn brown and green. In faint letters, the tag read Mede-Vail.

Special artist, indeed. I felt the shiver. Medieval Europe. Medever College. Two passions.

It had to be she. Back, after all these years.

Living on a farm, the last I'd heard. Tending cows. Raising chickens—she, with all her talent. Doing heavy work instead of coddling her golden hands. No more knit miniskirts turning up on friends or in local shops. No more newsboy hats or crocheted vests springing out on the first warm day. "Well, who wears that stuff anymore, anyway?" old friends sniffed, shrugging off the disappointment of it all.

Why did she have to run off, just as the rest of us were having babies? Needing fairylike layettes for presents, and damn the cost! Couldn't she have waited a bit longer?

But there'd never been any baby stuff from her needles. None of those kitchy-koo carry blankets, no booties. "Oh, I've never taken to pastels," she'd always said, "I like the colors of metal, the colors of blood, armies clashing in dead of night." And she was only half-joking. "If it's not cool, it's gotta be serious stuff," she'd add, in case we hadn't gotten the message.

"Have a look at this one." The salesclerk lifted it off the hanger carefully and turned it front and back, as though making passes before a bull. Lined with red satin, it was a red-and-black Venetian cape with a standing collar. Wools, ribbons, everything glistened in the dancing light.

"Mmm. Fabulous. Just needs a mask," I said.

"Yes. I'd wear this one myself. I'm quite certain it will appreciate in value as her work becomes better known. She's developing quite the reputation lately, and not just for her talent. For her expertise as well. She's very particular about the materials she uses. She keeps angora rabbits so she can harvest the hair. She knows the most obscure spinners, and she travels around the country for the yarn shows."

"Rabbits?" I said, perhaps to gain time, perhaps a little too snootily. Not quite what we would have expected.

"And she'll do commissions. Right now I know she's contemplating a bridal coat, if you know anyone who might be interested. The bride would have to be statuesque and she'd have to be a person who'd enjoy the drama of the work. I've seen some of the yarns. Gossamer shades of white and pale pale pink, you wouldn't believe how many. Fairy stuff, really, though to be honest, I can only see it being worn in winter."

I didn't say, *She must have changed, then. Those were colors she'd sworn never to use.*

I didn't say, *I used to know her.* A good friend, in faraway times and places. High school. University. Bridesmaids at each other's weddings. Then a less than good friend; then her flight; and then nothing. No contact, no word. Nothing for twenty years. But if I were now to put my mind to it, I could still go to tears.

Not just for her flight—that was bad enough—but for all the betrayals that had come before it. There had been crises in both our lives, and she had run from hers. Rightly or wrongly, we'd all felt a little sorry for her husband. Her first husband. Probably her only husband, since I don't think she'd ever married any of the others, and if rumor were true there'd been more than a few. I wondered whether she'd recently left one back on the farm.

"Would you like to meet the artist?" the salesclerk offered, reaching for a flyer. "We're having an opening reception this weekend."

Now she had me. Should I show up and surprise her? Should we do delighted "Emma, darling!" "Kathi, darling!" air kisses to satisfy the crowd? Or should I say, *I have to check my schedule?*

I wasn't sure she'd want to see me. I wasn't sure I wanted to see her.

Maybe I did. Maybe it was time.

I took the flyer. *We'll see.*

Those Who Bore and Nurtured Us: Foremother Knitting

Dropped Stitches

Helen Kay Polaski

Growing up in a big family has its merits. I learned early on that necessity is in fact the mother of invention. My mother could make a meal out of nothing for me and my fifteen siblings. She could whip up four bridesmaids' dresses in one week, cut any style of hairdo for a kid or adult of any age, and make splints out of Popsicle sticks for a baby bunny with a broken leg quicker than I could slurp up a second Popsicle.

My mother could do anything.

As a woodsman, my father wasn't around much. Don't get me wrong, he could do a lot of things, too. But he worked from dark to dark, so Mom was the one we went to whenever we needed help or an answer.

So, naturally, when I saw the UPS man delivering a box, I went searching for my answer-giver. As Mom rummaged through the box, she looked at me with that quick grin of hers. I smiled back.

"What's in it?"

"Oh, just a bunch of yarn," she answered.

Well, a bunch of yarn didn't seem all that important to me, but going by her smile, I figured I must have missed something. I asked who it was for. Her grin got even bigger as she pointed to herself, and extracted a letter from beneath the colorful skeins.

"Oh." I leaned forward and peered into the box as she opened the letter. Hundreds of different shades and colors of yarn snuggled together, practically begging to be touched. I reached into the box and drew out a multicolored skein. "Is it just yours?"

She grabbed me around the waist and tickled me. "Guess that depends what you need it for," she whispered happily. Then she cut off a length of pink yarn and helped me wrap it around my doll to keep the doll blanket from slipping off and shooed me out the door so she could read her letter in peace.

Getting a box of yarn was exciting, but getting the letter from Grandma was what really made Mom smile. As soon as she was finished reading it, she stuck it in her apron pocket and kept it with her. The yarn itself she shoved back in the box and put under her bed.

Over the years, we used yarn from that box for many things in our house. With twelve girls in the family, it came in handy whenever we were heading outdoors with our dolls. No one wanted a sick doll, and their blankets never fell off if they were tied on. We tied up Christmas presents with festive multicolored yarn. Yarn made great headbands in times of need. It also made excellent kite string. Heck, everything from cutting Velveeta cheese to playing cat's cradle came to pass without a hitch at our house because of yarn.

When I noticed Mom used it to tie the bottom cupboard door handles together to keep the baby from getting into something he shouldn't get into, my understanding of yarn grew accordingly. Not only was yarn great as an accessory to a toy or outfit, but it was a useful preventative, as well.

My older sisters used yarn to keep their boyfriends' rings from falling off their fingers, my younger sisters made jumping ropes out of braided yarn, and I made pom-poms for everyone's ice skates. Yarn found its way onto bamboo fishing rods, and at times replaced shoelaces.

Yarn also showed up at our house in the form of mittens.

Every year, Grandma knitted a wide variety of mittens for each of us. There were orange and purple mittens, pink and brown mittens, and yellow, green, and blue mittens. I vowed to do the same when I grew up.

But a life-altering event occurred when I was eighteen years old and put a damper on my knitting plans. I was living away from home for the first time. As winter drew nearer, I thought about Christmas and how different things were since Grandma had died some years earlier. She'd been the only knitter in the family. I decided to take up the slack. How hard could knitting be, anyway?

It started out fine. About a third of the way through my first mitten, I realized I'd dropped a stitch. I turned to my mother for advice on how to fix it.

"You'll have to ask someone else," Mom answered impatiently. "I don't know how to knit."

I was stunned to my core. Mom could do *anything*. Knitting had to be a piece of cake for her. After I got over my initial shock, I figured she was teasing me, so I bugged her incessantly. After a while, I even found myself getting angry. But the reality was she really *didn't* know how to knit. I asked why she'd never learned, and she said that knitting had been Grandma's job.

I know it was childish of me, but knowing that Mom couldn't knit made me not want to know, either. It left me feeling vulnerable and somehow different. Every time I looked at my knitting needles, a huge reality check hit. My mother couldn't do everything. Silly as it sounds, that scared me.

I put my needles away, never finished the mittens I'd started, never knit again.

Years later, I told Mom of my fearful moment and we shared a good laugh. She explained that she had been too busy making dinner, mending torn trouser knees, and cleaning to worry about making mittens. She'd expected to learn to knit from Grandma when she finally had time, but Grandma died suddenly in her early seventies. We had thought she'd be around for many more years.

Mom smiled her grin. "When I get old and you have all moved away and there aren't any grandchildren who need babysitting or feeding or attention at the moment, then I'll sit down and take over the job of knitting mittens." I agreed it sounded like a relaxing way to spend her old age.

But she didn't get to hang around until she was older. She died after a courageous three-month fight with cancer when she was sixty-five years old.

As I strolled through the Christmas aisles of a local fabric store last year, the fourth Christmas since we lost her, I thought about my mother and grandmother and the upcoming holidays. The holiday seemed very different, now that two of the most important people in our family were no longer with us. I started thinking about mittens and knitting needles and how good they'd felt in my hands for those few brief weeks, long ago.

I picked up several multicolored skeins of yarn and dropped them into my shopping cart. How many mittens could I knit before Christmas? As I rounded the corner and headed toward a wall covered with various sizes and types of knitting needles (most enticing!), I could feel a smile starting to tug at the corners of my mouth. It all suddenly made sense. Perhaps it was time I picked up my dropped stitches and carried on a tradition that should never have ended.

The Pink Bikini
Tara Jon Manning

When I was a little kid, my mom was always knitting—usually for me. She tells me that I would sit at her feet, watching her make each stitch, then give her directions as to just where a flower should be embroidered, or where a decorative patch should be sewn on one of the succession of hooded pullovers I am wearing in every picture ever taken of me. One spring, when I was about five, my mom put down her knitting needles and pulled out a crochet hook. It was 1972 and everyone was crocheting—granny squares, rainbow vests, and ponchos, just about everything you can imagine. My mom, being a product of her time, decided to make me a crocheted bikini just like the ones that supermodels wore on magazine covers.

I was so excited. I chose pink—a soft, powdery pink. I anxiously waited for the bikini to be finished and for the New Jersey spring to make way for the warm days of summer. As she pulled loops through loops to make up the two tiny rectangles for the top, and the swim-trunk-style pants, I sat at her knee and heard her talk about how adorable the bikini was and what a wonderful summer was on the way.

Finally, it was done! It wasn't quite June, but it was warm enough for my mom to give in to my pleadings and let me try out my new suit. We drove some time to a small lake in the middle of the woods, I think it was in a state park near our home. I had proudly put my suit on at home and wore it in the car on the way, my sweaty thighs sticking to the vinyl upholstery of our family car. I wore only a light shirt as a cover-up.

The lake—more like a pond, really—was populated mainly by fishermen, middle-aged men drinking beer in aluminum boats, enjoying the first weekend of sun. It was a warm day, but there were few bathers at the muddy beach.

My mom and I found a great spot, near the water's edge, where she could watch my little round body splash in the water in my new pink bikini. I was so excited, and so shy! I usually wore tank-style suits to go swimming and I felt extremely self-conscious as I took off my shirt. My mother had to coax me into the water. The bikini was so magnificent that I screwed up my courage and walked to the water's edge.

Suddenly, the breeze turned cool. The water was freezing! I

pushed on, wading into the lake, until my shoulders were submerged. After about three minutes, I yelled to my mom, "It's cold!" and she called to come back and warm up in the sun. I waded toward the shore and began to walk out of the water.

But as I emerged, I realized my little pink bikini, heavy with water, was growing, stretching, beginning to slide. . . . In an instant, the bottom was gone, sunk to the muddy bottom of the lake. The top now hung around my hips, the straps skinny and about 2 feet long. I looked to my mom with what must have been an expression of sheer terror—and she was trying so hard not to laugh. I was distraught. My bikini! Half was forever sucked into the slime, the other now dangled from my shoulders, unbearably heavy. And I was freezing. I went completely hysterical. I was naked, and all the fishermen in their boats were staring. I didn't realize it was because I was sobbing so loudly; I thought they were laughing at me, looking like a fool in the wreck of my beautiful bikini. This eternity—which likely lasted all of about thirty seconds in real time—ended when my mother, still trying to keep her cool, scooped me up and wrapped a sandy towel around my shivering body. The outing was over. All I wanted was to go home. I had had my first taste of utter humiliation. The agony continued on the ride home, because (remember!) the pink bikini and the thin cover-up shirt were the only clothing I had with me. I rode all the way home with my bare bottom wrapped in an itchy, sand-covered towel.

About a week or so ago, I was walking through a crafts fair with my family. My son, who is five, wanted to look at everything. We moved from tent to tent, each filled with beautiful jewelery, metal sculpture, and fiber arts. As we rounded a bend, my husband stopped dead in his tracks and with a mischievous grin said, "Oh no! Turn around! Don't look." At the next booth, headless black acrylic mannequins displayed crocheted bikinis. A little girl was inspecting them closely. As my son dragged me on to the next shiny thing that had caught his attention, I kept myself from yelling out at her, "No, don't buy it! They're evil." In that instant, I had a small epiphany; I realized the pink bikini is why, while I love to knit, I will never, ever, be a crocheter.

A Different Time
Kay Dorn

At the bottom of my hope chest, wrapped in soft, worn sheets, lies a treasury of knit afghans, lace-edged pillowcases, a crocheted tablecloth, and tatted doilies. They have rested there, underneath my treasury of Nonna's handwork, for fifty-two years.

No, that's not exactly true. Once, in early 1960, those pieces came out for a few days, but then they returned to the bottom of the cedar chest. I will leave a copy of this story with them, so that when Mildred and I are gone, my children will know what to do with them.

In our large Italian family, Mildred and I were the only female cousins, and so my grandmother made it her business to produce a dowry for each of us. If we remarked on the beauty her hands were creating, with no pattern in sight, she would smile and say, "*tua dote*" (your dowry).

The two collections weren't exactly the same. The knit afghans are colorful but contrasting. Whereas Mildred's crocheted tablecloth is pinwheel stitch, mine has a pineapple pattern. Her doilies are tatted in a lacy circle, whereas mine are soft linen, hand-hemmed, then worked around the edges. But in number they are identical. Particularly remarkable are the guest towels with a thread meticulously pulled through to make a new weave in color. I think Nonna must have attached the colored thread to one of the existing threads of the weft and carefully pulled it through the warp of the woven linen. Such patience—and all this with failing eyesight!

Unfortunately, fate took a hand just after Mildred graduated from high school. She fell in love and became pregnant. The term then was "She had to get married." She delivered a healthy boy who has grown to be a caring and happy family man.

But Nonna never acknowledged Mildred's plight. Although our grandmother was a generous, loving person, the phrase "unwed mother" was not in her vocabulary. I can still see the sad ritual during which she lifted the hinged reed lid of the big rectangular basket that had held her blankets on the ship from Italy, carefully removed Mildred's collection, and deposited it in the round basket that contained my *dote*. Nothing was said aloud, but all the aunts knew and whispered about it.

Mildred knew, too.

Later, when I was married, the basket holding the duplicate dowries went with me to my new home. I wrapped Mildred's *dote* in the same soft worn sheets that hold them now and put them in the bottom of my hope chest.

Then, years later, after Nonna died, I decided it was time.

I took Mildred's linens from their niche, put them back in

the big rectangular basket, which I had saved all those years, and brought them to her.

"I've brought you a present," I announced when she answered the door. Her face lit up. But the second she saw the basket and what it held, tears came to her eyes and she shook her head violently. "I never want to see those again."

Maybe what I did was insensitive. It hadn't occurred to me that, after all those years, she would still feel the hurt. But there it was on her face, as fresh as the day I had found her crying because Nonna wouldn't go to her wedding. I put Mildred's *dote* back in the bottom of my cedar chest, and neither of us ever mentioned it again.

But now that I'm older and I'm starting to distribute some of my own treasures, I feel I need to face it once more.

That's why I have written this piece, which I will leave with Mildred's *dote*. My children will read it after we are both gone and will know to give Nonna's handwork to my cousin's grandchildren. And they will treasure the linens crafted so lovingly by their great-great-grandmother so long ago. Although they are young now, later they will understand, I'm sure, that Nonna lived in a different time and that she did what she felt she had to do. I know that that caring woman never suspected how deeply she hurt her beloved granddaughter.

If this all happened today, and Nonna were still alive, it would be different. I'm sure that she'd be joyously sitting in her Morris chair, knitting a blankee for her very first great-grandchild.

Or so I hope.

With Relish

Hannah Treworgy

My grandmother died last year. She was ninety-three. She was good at a lot of things: listening, bookkeeping, crocheting and knitting, and making zucchini relish. She would make relish every summer. The neighbors brought her zucchini by the basketful, hoping to be remembered with a jar or two at the end of the canning season. I visited Nana every couple of months, and every time she would tell me to take as many jars as I wanted home with me. That generosity sums up my grandmother's spirit, because she always ran out of relish months before the next zucchini was ready, with a list of waiting recipients already a page long.

The problem was that I didn't really like zucchini relish. Every family recipe, from tuna salad to Thanksgiving stuffing, included generous amounts of the sweet yet vinegary stuff. It was my family's secret ingredient, our secret weapon. We had so much relish that we could dump an entire jar into a casserole without blinking an eye. And, yet, even with genetics and accessibility on my side, I was not a fan; I wouldn't even eat food that had the relish in it. Every jar that I casually brought home, I would then give away to a friend. And so it went for years, as I shared my grandmother's bounty with countless appreciative acquaintances.

Nana never did anything halfway. The extent of her relish

making was exceeded only by the volume of her knitting. She always had a huge spool of cotton yarn next to her chair in the TV room, along with a pair of number 9 needles. She would knit a dishcloth every night, start to finish, while watching ancient BBC comedies or Nascar racing. Every night. After weaving in the last dangling end, she would fold each finished cloth in quarters, put it in a Ziploc bag, and drop it in a basket on the other side of her chair. Each visitor who stopped by— and there were many—heard "Take a dishcloth from the basket on your way out. I've got so many I don't know what to do with them!" The dishcloths I did like; I took one every time I went for a visit. Once I asked Nana to show me how to knit; I imagined myself churning out dishcloths, scarves, maybe even socks for my impressed and astonished friends. But I got so confused by the knitting and purling (forget about a yarn-over!) that I gave up almost immediately. I decided to leave the knitting to the real knitters, like my grandmother, my mother, and my older sister, Sarah.

Mum and Sarah are crazy yarn-freak knitters. They spit out sweaters as easily as Nana made dishcloths. A few years ago, they planned a two-week camping trip to Nova Scotia to visit yarn shops and sheep farms. Although I am much more comfortable with room service and central air-conditioning, I packed up my laptop and went along. We had a great time. I have the pictures to prove it: Mum and Sarah digging through piles of yarn, me sitting outside the shop with my computer and the dog. The best part about it, however, was the time we got to spend together. Every night we would set up the tent, then sit around a campfire and just talk. Mum and Sarah would knit, and I would poke at the fire with a stick. I felt pretty comfortable in my role as fire poker, but I was getting a little envious of the yarn talk that I was not part of. We talked about books and the things we had done and seen so far, but their excitement over yet-to-be-realized sweaters, vests, and socks had me feeling a little bit the outsider.

A couple of days before it was time to head home, I decided to give knitting another go. Instead of staying outside with the dog, I actually went inside a knitting shop. I found a project that Sarah swore even I could do: a hat, on circular needles. No purling, no yarnovers. Just straight knitting, she said. My mother eagerly bought the supplies for me. That night, as I sat between the two of them, the three of us around the campfire, I finally learned how to knit. My older sister, who had taught me the alphabet and how to swear, was now patiently casting on eighty-eight stitches, explaining how each loop of yarn is essential to a hat. I felt such a sense of belonging. We sat, we chatted, we knit. Such purpose, such contentment.

Then we went home. Since I was still at the beginning of my project, I had problems. I dropped stitches, and there was no one there to hand my work to and say "fix this, please." I was kicking myself for all the time I'd wasted. I had had two patient and loving knitting teachers at my disposal, and I'd spent my time playing on the computer instead of learning from them. Eventually, though, I figured out how to get out of my knitting quandaries myself.

I still bring my knitting to family gatherings so I can recapture that feeling of belonging, and it works. Although I did *almost* miss having that special time with my sister and mother, I didn't miss it altogether. And I guess that's what really matters.

I am so grateful that I knew my grandmother for thirty-one

years. She was such a light in my life, and I miss her terribly. She made her last batch of relish last summer. After she passed away, I was feeling especially empty one day. I opened the one jar of her relish that I had kept for myself, and tried a bit. It was delicious.

The Reminder
Kathryn Eike Dudding

Once there was a mother who knit for her daughter. She started knitting for the daughter even before the daughter was born: baby bonnets and booties and sweaters. After the daughter was born, the mother knit sweaters and scarves and hats, sometimes a cap to cover the daughter's entire head, sometimes an ear-warmer—a narrow rectangle going from ear to ear and tying under the chin.

Once the mother made mother-daughter sweaters in yarn that matched the daughter's eyes. Unfortunately, the mother made the daughter's sweater first. By the time the mother finished her own sweater, the daughter had outgrown hers. But every time the mother wore that sweater, they both were reminded of the daughter's matching sweater.

One day, when the daughter was nine, she asked, "Mommy, will you teach me how to knit?"

The mother smiled. "I'd be happy to teach you to knit. I've been hoping that you would ask."

So the mother taught the daughter how to knit. First, the

daughter knit sweaters and dresses for her dolls. Then, she started making sweaters for herself, then for her father and brother, her fiancé, her husband, her son, and her friends. But she never made a sweater for her mother. The thought flitted through her mind once, but she quickly dismissed it. "Whenever Mom sees a sweater she likes, she makes it for herself."

But the mother kept on making sweaters for the daughter. The last thing the mother knit for her daughter was a red sweater with a pattern of raised hearts across the shoulders. Then the mother died.

The daughter wore that sweater many, many times. Every time she wore it, she was reminded of her mother. She began to regret that she had never made a sweater for her mother. She had made her mother other things, but never a sweater.

Finally, one day, that red sweater was worn out. There were holes at the elbows, a stain on one arm, and frayed yarn around all the edges.

"I don't want to throw this sweater away. It was the last sweater my mother made for me. Isn't there something I can do?"

She looked at that sweater long and hard. "Well, I could take the sleeves off and save the good yarn, then use that good yarn to mend the edges of the body. Then I'd have a vest to wear." So that's what she did, and there was just enough yarn to do it.

The daughter wore that vest many, many times. Every time she wore it, she was reminded of her mother.

Finally, one day, that red vest was worn out. There was a stain on one side and it was ratty around the edges.

"I don't want to throw this vest away. It's from the last sweater my mother made for me. Isn't there something I can do? Maybe I could take the vest apart, save the good yarn, and make something from that."

She ended up with a ball of good yarn about the size of a big cantaloupe. "Now, what can I make with this much yarn? I know, I'll make a scarf with a pattern of raised hearts on it." So that's what she did, and there was just enough yarn to make a scarf to keep her neck warm during the winter months.

The daughter wore that scarf many, many times. Every time she wore it, she was reminded of her mother.

Finally, one day, that red scarf was worn out. There was a hole in the middle and it was ratty around the edges.

"I don't want to throw this scarf away. It's from the last sweater my mother made for me. Isn't there something I can do? Maybe I could take the scarf apart, save the good yarn, and make something from that."

She ended up with a ball of good yarn about the size of a grapefruit. "Now, what can I make with this much yarn? I know, I'll make an ear-warmer with a pattern of raised hearts on it." So that's what she did. There was just enough yarn to make an ear-warmer to keep her ears warm during the winter months.

The daughter wore that ear-warmer many, many times. Every time she wore it, she was reminded of her mother.

Finally, one day, that red ear-warmer was worn out. There was a hole on one side and it was ratty around the edges.

"I don't want to throw this ear-warmer away, It's from the last sweater my mother made for me. Isn't there something I can do? Maybe I could take it apart, save the good yarn, and make something from that."

She ended up with a ball of good yarn about the size of a

lemon. "Now, what can I make with this much yarn? That's not very much yarn at all. I can't make anything to wear. I know! I'll make a Christmas ornament, a four-pointed star with a pattern of a raised heart in the middle." So that's what she did. Since it was still several months until Christmas, she found a box to put the star in and a piece of cedar to keep the star safe from moths. Then, she put the box with the rest of her Christmas ornaments in the attic. She knew that whenever she saw that ornament on her Christmas tree, she would be reminded of her mother.

The daughter had one 3-inch piece of good yarn left. "Is there anything I can make from this last little bit of yarn? Something I could use all year? I know that's a lot to ask from such a small bit of yarn."

She thought and she thought. And then the daughter smiled, because she was a storyteller as well as a knitter.

That last bit of yarn was just enough for the daughter to make this story for her mother. And the daughter knew that whenever she told this story, she would be reminded of her mother.

The Knitting Studio
Chris Mastin

To get to my mother's studio, I must first pass through my stepfather's office, with its piles of years-old papers, its unfinished projects, and its all-encompassing, wraparound desk.

The studio, by contrast, is a place of color and organization. The long narrow window in the far wall sheds filtered light onto walls of pale peach and aqua, onto white chairs with seats covered in a lighthearted coordinating cotton, and onto plastic boxes filled with blues, reds, rusts, greens, purples, and maroons—countless balls, cones, and skeins of yarn. Yarn and its accoutrements are everywhere, for this is a knitting studio, a place for my mother's obsession and delight. It is where I look first when I come to fetch her for our Saturday morning errands.

But my mother is not in her studio this morning. My step-father calls down from upstairs that she's out in the backyard tending her roses. I don't go outside right away. Instead, I take a long look around the room. My mother's faint rosewater scent mingles with the smell of dyed wool. Her presence is palpable here, even in her absence.

You might call this a small room, but to my mother it is barely a room at all. Instead, it is a place that gives her a sense of control, a haven from my stepfather's chaos of manner and thought and from his infirmity, a quiet center inside the uncertainty all around, and (most importantly) a place where creative visions come to life.

My grandmother and I both used to knit but gave it up, my grandmother because she made too many mistakes and I because I was too slow. My mother, though, revels in our end-less requests. She and I go to our Thursday night yoga class proudly wearing socks she has made. She likes to tell her knitting-guild friends that I claim to need a different sweater for each day of the year.

In the center of the studio is Mission Control: a white table. This is where she designs new patterns and knits existing ones. On it, laid out in a neat mosaic, lie backs, fronts, and sleeves of sweaters, in various stages of gestation—sweaters for herself, her family, and her clients. I marvel at the large green dragon with the orange-red tongue on the front of the sweater she is making for my nephew. A blue-green glass bowl holds stitch counters, stitch markers, and buttons. A small notebook and mechanical pencil wait to the right of the chair where my mother sits, for the notes she takes on her progress.

Beneath the window is her knitting library: books interspersed with magazines and patterns in periodical holders, all alphabetically organized by genre, from cardigans to hats to purses to socks. Canadian, Italian, Irish, French, American, Scandinavian, Peruvian. Knit, purl, DK, ST, YO, cast on, cast off, pick up, increase, decrease: an international language of hands and needles.

Along the west wall, floor-to-ceiling shelves bracket a large bulletin board. In the shelves are plastic boxes containing yarn: mohair, merino, rayon, Shetland, silk, cotton, microfiber, all organized according to her needs. On the bulletin board are tacked swatches she has knitted, experiments in pattern or gauge, and color photographs of beautiful sweaters by favorite designers. At the foot of the bulletin board stands a narrow Japanese vase filled with ornately carved but fully functional wooden needles of oak and bamboo.

Across from the table is an antique chest of drawers inherited from one of my stepfather's Texas relatives. The drawers belly out, a pregnancy in wood, created by someone with a romantic view of the mundane; they are in marked contrast to the straight lines in the rest of the room. This chest will go to my sister when our mother dies. On top sits an antique doll in a wire sleigh. My mother tells me that the doll's ringlets and pouty expression remind her of me as a child. I laugh now when she starts to singsong, "There was a little girl, with a little curl, right in the middle of her forehead," though I remember not being amused by it when I was young and in the middle of a tantrum. Next to the doll is a small black-faced sheep. Its crookedly embroidered nose and mouth make my mother laugh whenever she looks at it.

On the narrow wall between the doorway and the bathroom is a large oak-framed mirror for modeling my mother's creations. We stand in front of this mirror, she, I, and her clients, turning our heads this way and that, imagining times and places for wearing this sweater or that shawl or those socks or that purse.

It is very specific, this room. No visitor would stay here for long unless the visitor shared this fascination for colors and textures, liked to fondle soft yarns against a cheek. I linger because in this room I hear the things my mother cannot say aloud.

My mother tells me that one day she may have to give up this room. My stepfather's office and this studio, with its bathroom, could convert easily into a small apartment when my stepfather becomes confined to a wheelchair with advanced Parkinson's disease. Although she is not an overtly sentimental person, my mother's love for this room is obvious. I can tell that sometimes she wishes she could remain here forever, quietly focused on projects, protected from the strains of marriage to a man who is slowly and irretrievably unraveling.

Sweaters

Lesléa Newman

Every afternoon at 3:40 when Sarah got home from school, she found her mother sitting in the living room watching Oprah Winfrey, smoking a Marlboro Light, drinking a cup of instant coffee laced with Sweet'n Low, and knitting a sweater, all at the same time. Sarah could count on this as surely as she could count on the fact that she would never have straight hair or a turned-up nose or be described as "leggy." Some things, no matter how hard you wished they were different, always stayed the same.

Sarah made sure she used her special little key to disengage the burglar alarm before she unlocked the front door and stepped into the house. After dumping her school books and jacket on the front stairs, she dragged herself into the living room. And sure enough, there was her mother—Mrs. Edelman, as everyone, even Sarah, thought of her—in her pale yellow bathrobe and matching fuzzy slippers, slumped in her rust-colored recliner, surrounded by a cloud of blue-gray smoke, with two ivory-colored knitting needles in her hands, clacking away.

"Hi," Sarah said, but her mother was too busy silently counting stitches to reply. "Hey, Alfie, want to go for a walk?" Sarah asked over the blaring TV. The old cocker spaniel dragged himself out from under the extended footrest of Mrs. Edelman's chair and gave himself a good stretch, kicking out first his right hind paw and then his left, and bowing down until his chin touched the carpet. Sarah knew Alfie hadn't been out since seven o'clock that morning when she had taken him for a short walk before she left for school. She knew this not only by the way Alfie did his side-stepping I-really-have-to-go dance but also from the way her mother was dressed—or rather, not dressed. Mrs. Edelman would never set foot outside her front door in her bathrobe and slippers. She thought no one knew she sat in the house in her pajamas all day watching TV and knitting, but as Sarah knew her mother couldn't pull the wool over anyone's eyes. Not their neighbor Mrs. Maresco, who always asked Sarah, "How's your mom, dear?" in a voice devoid of real concern and filled with fake pity. Not her classmates, who, though they were kind and invited Sarah to their homes, never once asked why she never asked them over. And certainly not her father, who arrived home from the office later and later these days—six, seven, eight o'clock at night—only to find his wife already in bed. "Was she dressed when you got home today?" he'd ask Sarah, who answered with a quick shake of her head, wanting to dismiss the whole thing.

"Can you make me a cup of coffee before you take him out?" Mrs. Edelman nodded toward her mug without missing a beat, her knitting needles flapping up and down like useless wings.

Sarah took the cup and headed for the kitchen with Alfie at her heels. "You can wait, can't you?" she asked the dog, who looked up at her, his head tilted to one side. "Here, have some People Crackers." Sarah turned on the flame under the tea kettle and then dropped the fire fighter and police officer onto the linoleum floor. Alfie gobbled them with gusto while

Sarah dumped a spoonful of instant coffee into her mother's mug, tore open a pink packet of artificial sweetener, and then, when the tea kettle whistled, filled the cup with boiling water.

"What do you think?" Mrs. Edelman asked, lifting her knitting when Sarah and Alfie came back into the living room.

The sweater she was making looked the same as yesterday, only longer, though of course Sarah could never say that. She put her mother's coffee on an end table next to her chair and muttered, "It's nice," as she did every day during her mother's show-and-tell. "Who's it for?"

"I don't know yet," Mrs. Edelman said. This meant, Sarah knew, that the sweater would wind up in the guest room closet with its peers, which now numbered well over a hundred. The sweaters were all folded neatly and arranged precisely by color and size, "just in case," as Mrs. Edelman often told Sarah. Just in case of what, Sarah didn't know.

Sarah stood where she was for a minute and watched as her mother stabbed her cigarette out in an ashtray shaped like an upturned hand, lit a fresh one with a silver lighter, took a sip of her coffee, and continued to knit. Mrs. Edelman wrapped a strand of orange wool around her extended left index finger by twirling it around in a counterclockwise circle—the same gesture Sarah made at the side of her head to indicate to her friends that her mother was crazy—and then quickly raised her arms over her head and then lowered them. This movement stretched taut and then loosened the umbilical cord of wool that joined the knitting in Mrs. Edelman's lap to the ball of wool at her feet.

"After I'm done with this one, I'll make you a sweater," Mrs. Edelman said to her daughter. "What color would you like?"

"Black," Sarah answered.

"Black?" Mrs. Edelman sounded surprised, as though she'd never heard the word before, as though she and Sarah hadn't had this conversation a thousand times.

"It's my favorite color," Sarah reminded her mother.

"Black wouldn't work with the sweater I'm thinking about," Mrs. Edelman said. "How about if I make you a blue sweater?"

"I don't wear blue."

"How about red?"

"I don't wear red."

"Then yellow," Mrs. Edelman said, nodding her head as if the matter were settled.

"I don't wear yellow," Sarah said, raising her voice slightly as if her mother had suddenly gone partially deaf. "I want a black sweater."

"Sarah, Alfie really needs to go out." Mrs. Edelman pointed at the dog with her knitting and then slipped a stitch from the left needle onto the right. "And please use his leash."

"I will," Sarah said, even though she and her mother both knew she would unclip the leash from Alfie's collar the minute they stepped outside. And, as soon as she did so, Alfie ran to the nearest tree, lifted his leg, and then trotted back to Sarah so she could praise him.

"Good boy. Stay." Sarah thrust one hand out, palm down, so Alfie wouldn't move while she looked both ways. "Okay." She waved him across the street. "Let's go to the park."

Alfie trotted across the grass past the slide and the merry-go-round and then rolled on his back in a patch of sunlight while Sarah flopped belly-down onto a swing that barely held her weight. She twisted herself around in a circle until the chains that held the swing were tangled and taut. Then, lifting her feet, she let herself spin around in a dizzying circle, forgetting just for a moment that she was a teenager instead of a five-year-old.

After twirling around a few more times, Sarah sat rightways on the swing, used her legs to pump herself into the air, and thought about her mother. Did she really sit in the house knitting all day, or did she have some secret life Sarah couldn't even begin to imagine? How could somebody just sit and knit for eight hours a day? But what else would her mother do? She had been a knitter for as long as Sarah could remember. When Sarah was little, she liked to line up her mother's knitting needles, starting with the ones as skinny as the pick-up sticks she used to play with, all the way up to the ones as thick as the stick Alfie was now holding between his front paws and gnawing on. Sarah used to spend hours looking through her mother's knitting books, admiring the pretty ladies in their soft-looking sweaters that her mother could create like magic. And, best of all, Sarah had loved sitting in a chair facing her mother with her chubby little arms extended so Mrs. Edelman could wind the skein of wool her daughter was holding between her wrists into a perfectly round ball.

When Sarah was twelve, her mother had tried to teach her how to knit a scarf, but Sarah wasn't very good at it. The wool wrapped around her left index finger cut off her circulation. She kept dropping stitches. Half the scarf was too loose and the other half too tight. In the end, Mrs. Edelman ripped out the whole thing, wound the wool back into a ball, and used it to make a pair of socks for Sarah's father.

"C'mon, Alfie." Sarah dragged her feet in the sand to still her swing and stood up. "Time to go home and make supper."

When Sarah and Alfie got back to the house, Sarah paused at the front door to clip the dog's leash onto his collar even though she knew her mother would be locked up in her bedroom, "retired," as she put it, for the night. She fed Alfie his Alpo and then took out two frozen TV dinners for herself and her father. At least there's always food in the house, thought Sarah, though she didn't know how it got there. Either her mother actually managed to dress herself and go to the store once a week, or (more likely) she called in her grocery order and had it delivered. In a few months, Sarah would be old enough to drive. She wondered if she would have to do the grocery shopping on top of everything else. Probably. Oh well, what did it matter? In a little over a year, she would graduate from high school and be shipped off to college. She wasn't sure whether she wanted to go or not, but according to her parents, the matter had already been decided. And what else would she do anyway, work at McDonald's? College was her ticket out, her eject button, her great escape.

When the time finally came for Sarah to leave, she went as far as she could, to a school clear across the country in southern California. Sarah's classes were full of blond leggy girls with ski-slope noses who had no idea she had a crazy mother. Or a mother at all, since she never spoke about her. "I was raised by wolves," Sarah joked whenever asked, and then a look came over her face that said very clearly she did not want to discuss it. Her two best friends, who were also from the East Coast, talked endlessly about their mothers and how they missed them, even though they spoke to them on the phone practically every day and received care packages on a regular basis. Once a month, Terry's mom sent a coffee can filled with homemade chocolate chip cookies, which her daughter proudly shared. And Jackie's mother was always sending things to remind her daughter of New England: tiny glass bottles shaped like maple leaves and filled with real maple syrup in the fall; a jar of blueberry preserves they'd bought on a hiking trip to Maine the previous spring. Sarah's mother sent nothing.

Until the week before Thanksgiving.

As she always did, Sarah stopped at her mailbox on the way back to her dorm from her art history class. She was excited to see that she'd gotten a package, until she saw it was from her mother. What in the world could she have possibly sent her? Sarah put the package under her coat as if it contained weapons or drugs, or something else forbidden and dangerous, and made her way back to her room. She locked the door behind her and then contemplated the package. She didn't have to open it. But what was she so afraid of?

"It's not going to bite you," Sarah said aloud. She tore open the brown paper and lifted the top of the box. The smell of cigarette smoke filled her nostrils as she folded back two sheets of tissue paper and looked at the black sweater. "Oh my God," she whispered. A great sadness overtook her even before she saw what lay underneath the sweater: Alfie's leash and collar. Which could only mean one thing. Sarah's eyes blurred as she fingered the worn red leather that smelled of Alfie's fur. Tears spilled from her eyes as she pulled the sweater over her head, wrapped her arms around her waist and rocked herself back and forth, holding herself as though she were her own mother.

Things of the Spirit
part two

IN WHICH KNITTING COMFORTS US IN DESERT TIMES,
LEADS OUR THOUGHTS INTO INTERESTING PLACES,
AND BINDS US CLOSE TO GOD.

Hard Times: Through Thick, Thin, and Bouclé

How I Learned to Knit

Kathy Myers, as told to Lisa Quinto

The sound of my hard-soled shoes rang like cowbells
down the hushed hospital floor.
I was clutching my visitor's pass like gold,
afraid I'd lose it and not be allowed to see Lisa.
I'd never been in a mental hospital before.
I passed door after door until I finally found
the unit optimistically dubbed TRANSITIONS.
Out of habit, I reached for the doorknob—
of course, it was locked. A nurse buzzed
me in, and the explosion of white hurt my eyes:

white walls, white floors, a white bench next to
the white nurses' station. I was terrified.

Lisa was in with the doctor. I looked for someplace
to sit while I waited. There were so many rules that
I was afraid I'd break one or two or six thousand
and get tossed out. That white bench by the nurses'
station looked pretty safe. I sat down next to a small, gray-
    haired lady in a light blue jogging suit.
Her shoelaces were missing.
Everyone's shoelaces were missing. ("So we can't hang
ourselves," she explained.) I didn't want to
bother her, but she didn't look too dangerous, and besides,
she was knitting and I wanted to know what she was
    making.
"Just knitting to pass the time, hon," she said. "I spend a
    lot of time here."
I think her name was Mary, but from then on,
I called her the Yarn Lady. Watching her,
I felt the knot in my stomach begin to ease. It was
like magic: You take a big ball of yarn and, all of a
sudden, it's a sweater! Just what I needed in
my life at the time: Chaos everywhere, but here was a
predictable outcome.
I wanted to know if she could show me how to do that,
    too.
"Go buy some knitting needles and some yarn and come
back tomorrow morning," she instructed.

I returned the next day with my pink plastic knitting
needles and a garbage bag full of yarn; the nurses laughed

as they searched it, wanting to know whose
body was inside. I couldn't help it—I was a long way from
    home
and terrified that I'd run out of yarn and have to sit
there, waiting in that scary corridor with nothing to do.

The Yarn Lady was happy to see me again.
She said she had a husband and son, but they never
came to see her. Fifteen minutes later, I was
bumbling through my first knit and purl. We
sat close, the Yarn Lady and I, so she could
adjust my hold on the needles now and then.
Soon, the yarn felt like it was singing in my hands.
It felt like the soft touch of a lover's body against my finger-
    tips—
soothing, relaxing, and completely natural.
"Come back next week and I'll teach you more,"
she said, smiling for the first time. "Go figure,
me teaching someone on the outside how to do
    something."

I sat with the Yarn Lady every weekend while Lisa
was there, but nobody ever came to visit her but me.
That made me sad. Learning to knit, however,
changed my life forever and came to be an almost
spiritual part of my existence. I hoped that someday, I too
could be a Yarn Lady. I lacked the words to thank her,
so the next weekend I showed up with a present.
It was just a book of knitting patterns, nothing special,
but I really wanted to give something back to her.
I got there and she was gone.

I only hope she knew how much her gift, given to me in the heart
of a psychiatric hospital, meant to me.

Peace Blanket
Kathryn Gunn

Peace blanket . . . blanket of peace . . .

It was September 12, 2001, and I knew I needed to make something. I needed the comfort the way a child needs a security blanket. I did not know what I would make, but the urge to create something was overwhelming. It was as overwhelming as the shock and the worry of not knowing whether friends were safe.

I tried to write something. I could not. The piece I started didn't include enough people; it wasn't satisfactory. Finish knitting a project? No, that wouldn't be the same. I had to *begin* something and it had to involve other people. Could I combine the two? How do you knit something you have written? How do you knit words for peace?

I went to online knitting lists and asked members to provide me with words they knew for *peace*. It was one way of involving friends and strangers, at home and overseas. Soon I had plenty of words for *peace* in other languages. I charted them out and put the Blissymbol for *peace* in between. Blissymbols make up an international nonspoken language, and the symbol for *peace* has the visual meaning *opposite war*, which seemed particularly appropriate. Charting out the work took days and nights. But again, I got help.

I used wool from my stash, wool I'd saved for another project that now seemed much less important. I chose white and blue, colors of peace. I started knitting on the morning train into the city. By the end of that first journey, three people had each added a stitch. That was a trial run. I thought the idea would work.

So I set out on some more journeys, many journeys. I took the blanket everywhere. When people asked me what I was doing, I told them, "I'm making a blanket for peace. If you know how to knit I'd be very pleased if you would add a stitch. If you don't know how to knit and would still like to do it, I'll help you."

People added stitches. They walked down the aisles of buses and railway carriages to make stitches. A bus driver stopped me as I was about to alight from his bus. He added three stitches, saying, "I've knitted my own socks for years." A three-year-old boy, guided carefully by his mother, put in a stitch. A 101-year-old woman put in an entire round, saying, "We need this. We need peace."

I did my turn of duty at the information booth for our guild at a quilting and crafts show, and people who stopped to look added stitches and sent other people over to add stitches. A developmentally delayed teenager put in a stitch for herself, and then, because her caregiver could not knit, put in a stitch for her caregiver as well. Some people made mistakes I left most of them. We are not perfect, and I did not want to make a perfect blanket; I wanted to make a shared experience.

Everywhere I went, people kept adding to the peace blanket. It reminded me of the way people pass the peace in church and of the peace greeting I was given in a visit to a synagogue. I told this to a Muslim woman as she added a stitch, and she added two more, "one for Christians and one for Jews."

When I had twenty words for peace, I stopped. By then, I had involved more than two hundred people. I hope, I think, we shared something important. We had created something.

My father eventually added his "stitch" by making a rod to hang the blanket from, and it went on display at the guild's biennial exhibition. When people who heard the story wished they had been able to add a stitch, I told them they had— merely by expressing the wish. Then I took it to the local library and they raffled it to raise money for more "words of peace." One of the Internet listers put the pattern on the Web for all of us to share.

And me? I feel a little better now. I have a photograph of the blanket to remind me of how we came together and passed the peace.

What Goes Around Comes Around
Sondra Rosenberg

In 1943, we were living in London, refugees from Hitler's invasion of Austria. I was seven. We had come to England from a fairly well-off life in prosperous Vienna with not much more than the proverbial clothes on our backs, and though both my parents worked when they could, jobs were scarce and money, as a result, uncertain. What they managed to earn was budgeted mainly for necessities such as food and rent.

Much of our clothing came from Jewish relief agencies in London's Whitechapel district. They operated on the honor system. People went in, took what they needed, and later returned what they could no longer use. Business was brisk, and we were among the beneficiaries. Also, my mother loved to knit and was very good at it. She kept the three of us in sweaters and scarves during the long, cold London winters when coal was scarce and central heating unheard of. An expert recycler, she could turn my outgrown sweaters into mittens or socks, or patch a worn sleeve as good as new.

One day, my mother returned from one of her periodic forays into Whitechapel with a large blue woolen dress. The color—bright, almost shimmering periwinkle—was a striking departure from her usual choices. Ever practical, she preferred colors that didn't show dirt. Washing clothes, like bathing, required handfuls of shillings to feed the hot-water meter in our cold-water flat. Unlike bathing, washing clothes was something that one could, with care, make an infrequent occurrence.

The dress was worn and shapeless, but viewed with my mother's canny, experienced eye, it had possibilities. It was handknit. She unraveled it. There turned out to be a lot of good wool left in that garment, enough for a dress for me, even one with long sleeves.

My mother took my measurements. She planned to make the dress too big for me, so that I'd have "room to grow into it." My mother reasoned that "a little bit too large" would gradually become "just right." My wearing it until it was just past "a little bit too small" would double the garment's life expectancy, however it might offend my fashion sense.

As children wore uniforms to school in England, the dress was to be reserved for special occasions such as going to synagogue, visiting on holidays, and receiving guests, mostly old friends from Vienna who had reached London after harrowing experiences.

My mother's needles began their rhythmic clicking one evening as we listened to the BBC. While Allied bombers undertook the destruction of Berlin, the dress took shape. When it was finished, it was indeed too big, but wearable. We cinched in the too-large waist with a belt, which also had the effect of shortening the hem. The too-long sleeves were rolled or pushed up according to my mood. I wore that dress with pride.

Eventually, I grew into it—almost. For some reason, my body did not quite expand according to my mother's plan. My arms grew more slowly than the rest of me, and when the dress fit my torso, the sleeves were still too long. By the time the sleeves fit properly, some two years later in 1945, the rest of the dress was much too short and much too tight. As it was still wearable as a dress, and as I had more than enough scarves and mittens, my mother decided not to morph it into another kind of garment but instead turned it back to the relief agency in Whitechapel.

In 1947, my parents and I emigrated to the U.S. We lived in New York, where I was enrolled in a Hebrew school along with other European refugees. A new girl entered my class. Her name was Helen, and she had recently arrived from England. We compared notes and found that we had lived fairly near each other in London.

After school one day, her mother and eight-year-old sister arrived to take her home. Helen introduced us, and chills ran up and down my spine.

Helen's sister was wearing my periwinkle blue dress! It had to be my dress; there couldn't be two dresses like that in the world.

I ran home to tell my mother, but she was skeptical. She didn't believe in coincidences, and besides, she reminded me, lots of women knit during wartime. I described the dress in detail and she conceded, somewhat reluctantly, that it did sound like my dress. Further than that, she was never willing to go.

I, however, was—and am—convinced. I'm sure that was my dress. It *had* to be my dress.

How did I know?

Because the dress fit Helen's sister perfectly, with one exception: The sleeves were too long.

To Knit or Not to Knit
Dana Snyder-Grant

My older sister was expecting her first child in the summer of 1985; her due date was August 18. We knew it was a boy, and I wanted to knit him a baby blanket. In May, I bought skeins of soft aqua-colored yarn.

I hadn't knit anything for several years before sitting down with this project. My mother had taught me to knit when I was a child, but I was never an accomplished knitter. I knit my father a scarf when I was about ten. "It was very long and skinny and not of much use," my mother says, "or maybe it was a misshapen sweater." So much for my skill. But, when I was a teenager, I did succeed at making colorful scarves that triumphed as gifts, or at least I thought they did. At age twenty-nine, I figured I could make a simple baby blanket.

There was a catch, however. I had been diagnosed with multiple sclerosis in December 1981. MS is an unpredictable but nonfatal disease of the central nervous system. Functions such as seeing and walking become uncontrolled because messages to and from the brain don't get through correctly. Since my diagnosis, I had had several flare-ups of the illness. For a few weeks, I'd experience lack of coordination or balance, difficulty walking, and impaired vision, all with extreme fatigue. These episodes were scary; I could become unable to walk or lose my vision entirely, or none of these things could happen.

I had the "relapsing-remitting" form of MS, and still do, but that phrase was misleading. During a flare-up in May 1983, I had lost my coordination. My hands felt like boxing gloves and I could not tie my shoes or write my name. Now, two years later, even "in remission," I still had difficulty writing. The fluid pen strokes I made when rested became a jerky scrawl when I was tired. Ah, these were the "residual" symptoms which my neurologist had described.

Even as I accepted the reality of MS, I often felt fine. The support of my friends and family sustained me. My physician's optimism rubbed off on me. During my most desperate times, I heard her words, "This too shall pass." She had no idea if my MS would progress rapidly, but statistics gave us hope. Two-thirds of people with MS are still walking twenty-five years after their diagnosis.

Living with chronic illness is about making choices about how to respond to the problem. When weary, I could either trust my judgment and rest, or ignore my gut and skip my nap. I was dealt a lousy hand of cards, but how I played them was under my control.

With anxiety and excitement, I chose to begin a program in social work in September 1984. I loved the work. The fatigue that is the hallmark of MS slowed me down and demanded that I pace myself, but I managed to keep up with my studies.

In July 1985, I had just completed my first year of school and was recovering from a mild episode of blurred vision. I had begun the baby blanket in June but had to put it aside because of my visual problems. Knitting did not come easily. It was not just that I had lost fine motor skills. Over the last few years, I had discovered that the simplest tasks could enervate me—cutting an apple, reading a newspaper, even watching television. The damage to my optic nerve from episodes of double vision meant that using my eyes for anything might exhaust me. My eyes could become heavy and tight. We don't realize how much sight orients us to the world until we start to lose it.

I had begun to rest my eyes periodically by closing them in order to avoid stimulation. At school, when tired, I would lie down on a couch with my eyes shut between classes. Afterwards, my eyes would return to normal. I learned quickly that knitting is not just about manual dexterity. We use our eyes, too.

My neurologist told me that people with MS use ten times

the energy that other people do to conduct their nerves' messages. No wonder knitting exhausted me! I would knit 2, purl 2 for ten minutes, and then need to lie down for five. But, dammit, I was determined to finish this blanket for the first child of the next generation.

That summer's flare interrupted me briefly, but when the symptoms remitted, I resumed work on the blanket. I wondered if my vision and fine motor skills would allow me to finish it.

At that point in my life, I didn't know if I would ever have children of my own. Between MS and graduate school, I had little time to pay attention to the dating scene. And children? If and when I met my mate, MS fatigue would cause me to think long and hard about that prospect. But I was excited by my sister's pregnancy. She had not hesitated about her decision. As I began to knit again for her baby, I wove the excitement of anticipation and a feeling of tenderness for mother and child into each stitch. I knit slowly but diligently.

We welcomed Benjamin into the world on August 27, 1985. I was still knitting.

That fall, classes resumed. Time and energy were at a premium. But perseverance and patience won out. On Thanksgiving 1985, I presented the blanket to Ben and his parents. It was so much more than a blanket to me. It was a triumph of body and soul.

It is eighteen years later, and I haven't picked up knitting needles since. But as I write this story, I've decided to try to knit again. I want to rediscover the skill and how it affects me. It's like riding a bicycle, I tell myself. Some things you just never forget. My hands know the motions well. Cast on, put needle in the stitch, lift arm, bring yarn over and toward me, and pull needle through. But my arms feel heavy; my eyes fatigue quickly. I recognize that I have made a choice. I will no longer knit, even though I am still able.

I have a good life as a psychotherapist, writer, and speaker, with a husband, good friends, and two cats. Benjamin is about to go away to college and I still have a skein of the aqua yarn. Sometimes I use the yarn as a cat toy, or to mend a sweater, darn a sock, or wrap a present.

But far more important, I save the yarn to remind me of what is possible.

The Whole World in My Hands
Dayna Macy

November 27, 2001. "This is how you cast on," chirps the effervescent salesclerk. I'm taking my first knitting lesson. In the wake of September 11, I am looking for some measure of peace and calm and am hoping I can find it in working with my hands. I am looking for a way to put the omnipresent news of the war behind me. I want to keep my hands busy. I cook. I change diapers. And soon, I'll knit.

Knitting is one of those things you think you might learn someday, but usually the time isn't quite right· There's too much other stuff to do. But after watching the World Trade Center collapse on TV in two thunderous sobs, I decided the time was right, right about now.

"And this is how you knit," says my teacher, a very short

woman with wire-frame glasses. She is so enthusiastic I wonder if she thinks knitting can save the world, one stitch at a time. I'm hoping it can. She puts one needle behind the other, wraps the yarn around the second needle, and loops the needle through. I watch her hands speak this foreign language. They move slowly, assuredly. Nice, even, plump stitches emerge from her work. "Here, you try."

My fingers are clumsy, their movements awkward. She cheers me on. My needles click, and I smile at the picture of this new homespun me. When I was younger, I tried on various identities, hoping one would eventually fit. But none of them featured me as a knitter.

"Ouch!" I yell as I stab my finger with a needle.

"Well," says my teacher, "knitting does keep you *present*."

I want to punch her sanctimonious snout, but her earnestness stops me. I don't want to be present. I want to forget. I am hoping knitting will help me forget. I want to knit through my fears, through my anxiety. And I want to create something tangible for my children, something to hold on to in this shaky world.

That night, I put my two-year-olds to bed. Matthew looks at me through his crib slats and says, "Sit, Mama." I get my knitting and sit on the rocking chair. "Mama knitting," Jack says.

I start counting—purl 5, knit 5, purl 5, knit 5. I admired this pattern on a sweater in the knitting store, and the teacher assured me it would not be hard. But somehow this row has only four stitches left where there should be five. And I dropped a few stitches three rows back. Do I rip the rows out and try to make the scarf perfect, or keep going?

I begin to feel agitated. Why did I pick this pattern in the first place? It's tedious and it's bugging me. I have to keep counting knit 5, purl 5, for what seems like an eternity, because this damn scarf I've committed to is three skeins long. Well, I think, at least I'm agitated about something other than the war.

I hear the quiet sounds of my children's breathing and know they're asleep. I sit in this dim room, with my knitting on my lap, rocking. I can't quite believe how much love fills these walls. How it all feels authentic and hard-won. I feel incredibly lucky.

I decide to keep knitting so I can feel this grace a little longer. This nursery feels warm and safe. I don't want to think about the war. Or my nagging suspicion that what is good and beautiful in this world can be gone in an instant. I don't want to think about the war, but I do. I think about other mothers halfway around the world trying to feed emaciated children. I think about mothers throwing themselves on top of their children to save them from American bombs. I see the hijackers' faces and I imagine myself shooting them point-blank between the eyes.

I knit faster to keep these thoughts at bay, but it's not working. Jesus! What does it take to calm me down? How can I feel at home in this new world?

So far, knitting isn't fun. And it isn't keeping the outside world from coming in. But I'm not ready to give up. My nascent scarf looks like a doll's blanket, but it will grow. I can already see the beginnings of the checkerboard pattern I liked so much in the knitting store. I run my hands over its short body and the wool feels warm. In the pumpkin yarn I notice flecks of deep raspberry. I imagine that one day it will be a fine scarf and will look especially nice against my old chocolate brown suede coat.

People all over the world know what it's like when war hits home. But I never did. Not until now. Now every time I hear a strange, loud sound, I look up at the sky and wonder. I open the newspaper, afraid to read more bad news. I want to stick close to home. My world feels much less safe than it did before, and things much less certain. In this new normality, and in the most cosmic scheme of things, I have no certainty that I will be able to keep my children safe. It was all an illusion anyway. September 11 just put the final stamp on it.

I imagine the sweaters I will make one day for Jack and Matthew, when I'm a much better knitter than I am now. I picture great, funnel-neck sweaters—tomato red on the outside and mustard yellow on the inside. I think of my children wearing them. I hope there is time enough to make them.

What Does Knitting Have to Do with War?
Nilda Mesa

Since I was eight years old, I've knit. Some years I knit a lot, some years hardly at all.

Since 9/11, I've knit a lot. More than ever, maybe even more than those other years combined. I'm not the only one—they say knitting is hot, "the new yoga," and that stars like Julia Roberts do it, too. Here in jittery New York City, knitting connects me to Nana, who taught me, her favorite grandchild, to make doll clothes when her own daughters had better things to do.

So last week, home sick with a cold and bored out of my mind, I did what many other knitters today do: I browsed eBay. I found rare knitting books that have shot up to five hundred dollars, checked out yarns from Turkey and Italy, and poked around the knitting patterns. I looked at lacy Victorian patterns from the 1860s, and "mod" patterns from the 1960s. Buxom bobbed models sported flapper styles, and big-haired models thrust out their 1980s shoulder pads.

Then I stumbled upon a different listing: KNIT FOR DEFENSE RED HEART WWII 1941. In World War II, knitters supported the war effort by making hats, gloves, socks, and scarves to warm the boys overseas. Given rationing, yarn was hard to come by. Women carefully unraveled sweaters, lovingly reknit the yarn, and sent their projects to the front lines. Yarn companies such as Red Heart published patterns to support the war effort. For a starting bid of four dollars, I could bid on this piece of history. I clicked.

Up popped a notice from eBay:

Dear User:

Unfortunately, access to this particular category or item has been blocked due to legal restrictions in your home country. Based on our discussions with concerned government agencies and eBay community members, we have taken these steps to reduce the chance of inappropriate items being displayed.

The notice offered an apology and invited me to find "other items of interest."

In the Clinton administration, I was a political appointee at the Pentagon, and came to admire and deeply respect my military colleagues. Along the way, I'd seen some interesting security classifications (though, in fairness, not many). But a *knitting pattern*?

Thinking there must be some mistake, I tried to bid on the item again. Same notice. There obviously were not many knitters at the Department of Homeland Security or the Department of Justice.

I called my friend Audrey, who is older than I and was a knitter when she had young kids. She remembered the World War II knitting circles and patterns. Her only explanation for the eBay notice was that maybe the patterns could be used by enemies to impersonate American soldiers. "With woolen hats and gloves in the Iraqi desert?" I asked. She gave up.

Thinking this was a fluke, I searched eBay again. Two other World War II patterns turned up, including HOW TO KNIT FOR VICTORY—WWII HOME FRONT. Both entries led to the same restriction notice.

Could it be that the patterns included suspiciously named stitches—the turret edging, broken arrow, or skyscraper pattern? Was it the brioche waffle stitch? Do cables have telecommunications capabilities? Could "cast off" be a coded communication?

A profound sense of loss sank in. When did my country decide to restrict sixty-year-old knitting patterns as threats to our national security, and what will be next?

It's hard to recognize this world anymore. I hope no one considers me a security risk if I include an Arabic cross pattern or Versailles edging on a sweater, or maybe these too will be renamed as the liberty cross or freedom edging.

And here I thought knitting was a refuge. . . .

Editors' Note

The puzzle explained: It turns out (as we learned from Nilda
Mesa later) that the eBay notice had a lot more to do with
World War II than it did with Iraq.

She and her husband spend several months a year in France
running a residency program for American artists in Brittany.
As a result, their Internet provider has given them a European code. In the European Union, and in France in particular, it is illegal to sell Nazi memorabilia, including anything
that may have a swastika on it, even if it's only in the background. To avoid European Union issues, therefore, eBay has
elected to cast a broad net, preventing people with European
codes from seeing almost any World War II material. Users
with American codes are not so restricted.

Nilda Mesa did manage to find a copy of the knitting booklet,
and it has no swastikas on it—only a photo of young U.S.
servicemen grinning bravely. It does make her wonder,
though, what will be restricted as the years go by.

In the Void
Marie Dorian

On Friday, November 21, 2001, I walked into the annual
meeting of the state governing board of the Virginia Organizing Project, held at the Tabor Retreat Center in Lynchburg,
Virginia. This statewide organization's goal is to work for social
change by giving those who traditionally do not have a voice

in their community the chance to make a difference. I had just been elected to the board a month earlier and was the youngest member there. I was surrounded by older, much more seasoned organizers who greeted each other with familiarity.

The chairs in the meeting room were arranged in a circle. I sat down next to Michelle, one of the only people there I knew. As I turned to talk to her, she pulled a gray mass out of a canvas bag. I watched, fascinated, as she rearranged the back of a pullover with small cables on bamboo needles. As she began to knit, a memory began to surface from my past.

I remembered sitting next to an older woman in a living room as she knit an afghan in browns and greens. A very ordinary business, with one difference: the purple and yellow bruises covering the right side of her face. This tranquil scene was taking place in a battered women's shelter, a place for women and children bruised like apples fallen from the tree and left to rot.

One night, three months earlier, my mother had fled with my two brothers and me to this place, where we hoped that we'd be safe. Since then, I had been a robot. My ten-year-old eyes saw horrors that continually played on an endless loop, whether I was waking or sleeping. By day, I went to school and tried to act as if nothing was wrong, ignoring the whispers behind cupped hands as I passed in the halls. But, at night, I lay in an unfamiliar bed and cried, tears running in rivers down my cheeks and into my pillow. The pain was so intense, I was starting to become detached from reality. I began to be increasingly withdrawn.

One night after a dinner of red beans and rice with sausage, I sat down next to a woman who had arrived the night before. I noticed that she was using two sticks to make loops that were connected to each other, and I watched as they built upon themselves. Caught up in the hypnotic rhythm, I felt the screams and thumps that chased me night and day receding. I sat there, mesmerized, for two or three hours, soothed by the rhythm of the needles.

Every day after school, I raced to the shelter to find the lady with the musical Creole accent, who drew me into her world of graceful motions, flicking the yarn with her left finger. She put the needles in my hands, guiding them with her own. The tactile experience of letting the wool glide through my fingers began to quiet my mind. We talked about Mardi Gras, the humidity, fresh hot beignets from Café Du Monde, ordinary everyday life in New Orleans. She told me stories of her childhood in northern Louisiana, of her brothers wrestling alligators, of trips to the farmers' market for merlitons and tomatoes and to the docks for shrimp. As I listened to her, I slowly began to open up. Stuttering and shaking, I told her of my mother being flung against the front door so hard that all the windows in the house shook. As long as the needles were in my hands, I was able to release all the violence I had seen. My tears became part of the fabric I was making, intertwined with the violence that had been knit into my life.

This wonderful woman left after six months, to start a new life in a place where she couldn't be found. I cried and clung to her, begging her not to leave. She gently disengaged me, and sat with me on our sofa. She explained to me that people will come in and out of my life as long as I live. But those who are important will be held next to your heart forever; they will always be a part of you. She said that for her, I was one of those people. After she left, it was if I locked away my memories of her because they were too painful to relive.

Now, as I watched Michelle knit, the memories all came flooding back, and I wanted to recapture that time in my life. I asked Michelle to help refresh my knitting skills. The next morning, when the board reconvened, I brought with me my first-ever needles and yarn. I relearned the fundamentals that weekend.

Now, every time I knit, I remember the woman with the soft Creole voice. I wonder if she remembers the lost little girl whom she brought back from the brink. She taught me that during the darkest nights of the soul, knitting can stand with you in the void.

What's Your Hobby?

Luke Shiffer

That question has plagued me for years. Not the intention behind the question—that's okay—but the simplicity of the question itself. Most people have an easy answer: Their hobby is whatever they do in their spare time. But for me, it's been more than that. What am I supposed to say? "I sit in front of the TV all day eating"?

It's not an acceptable answer to the question, though it's true. I'd once been a seventeen-year-old high-school kid who did absolutely nothing in his spare time, other than sitting in front of a flickering screen. I want to make one thing clear: I'm not a couch potato, whatever you may think. It's just that I have a void in my heart. And that void isn't going to be filled overnight. With my father in the military, and constant moving around, I never had the chance to set roots and make true friends. Nor could I spend quality time with my father—not enough, only a little.

And my parents began going through an ugly divorce. I would stay up long after midnight listening to them fight. Of course, my parents *never* put me in the middle of it, but when they fought, I felt a knife slash deep through my heart and out the other side. And the worst was still to come.

One evening, my brother and I were glued to the tube, escaping reality, when my mother came rushing into the room, her face flushed red. We made eye contact and I felt her terror go straight down my spine. A minute later, my father walked in, almost casually, as though everything was just fine. Then, right before our eyes, he came quietly up behind her and seized her slender neck. I felt as though I was watching an old movie. He was strangling her. He wanted only to end her life and his own pain.

He seemed to be looking right through me without seeing me, not taking in my obvious terror. I was only a kid; I didn't know what to do, what to think. This was my *father*. And he was jerking my mother around by the neck, like a child with a rag doll. It had to be a nightmare. It had to be. It would be gone by morning.

That was six years ago, but it might have happened hours ago. I still have terrifying dreams, deep into the night. I live that evening over and over again, every day.

If you'd asked me seven years ago what my hobby was, I would have said "playing ball with my dad." I'd hoped then to make him proud of me by playing professionally. Now I just want to forget it all.

But lately, I've found a new way of being. It started as a way of making use of the time I spent watching TV. Now, somehow, it's becoming a way for me to let go of the pain and turmoil, the guilt and the silence. I've found a group of friendly faces with whom I can be more open about the past. They're helping me grow. Slowly but surely, the pain is starting to fade and my heart has begun to live. Over the past few months, I've accomplished more than in the past six years. What started out as a way to max out my TV time grew into a method of letting go of my past. And, best of all, I've finally got an answer to that question that plagued me for years. Okay, it may not be standard teenage-boy stuff, but when people ask, "What's your hobby?" I answer with pride.

"Knitting."

Musings: Thoughts Flow as Yarn
Flows Through the Fingers

The Precognitive Knitter

Stephen Mead

Her hands sting a little
when lotion's applied, the knuckles
crackling, a couple of burnt bas-reliefs.
To touch them is to touch time, the mortal
immemorial ablaze from day one.
The bones within fingers, the tendons
and vessels shape the spine of some bird
testing its wingspan against a sun splay
of shadows. If held up to light,
they'd be ruddy and translucent, warm
as an embryo ultrasound-traced.

If held up in darkness,
they'd be an X ray of palm fronds,
unwithered, impervious.
Sure, she feels the cold easily,
yet she can also forecast a rainstorm,
such telepathy an ache, her namesake,
soothsayer??
—bright needles pulsing yarn
through the blackest of fabric,
a flower, firm and lovely. Later
the creation, even though stuck
in a closet, will brushfire bristle.
She knows this and knits gently.

A Glossary of Knitting
Zoë Blacksin

K: *Knit.* The knit stitch produces a fine, even fabric. Most of my life feels like knitting—fine and even. Days turn into weeks and weeks turn into months, like rows of little stitches, identical, blending into one another, creating one smooth swatch of time. As it falls off the needle, each stitch, viewed closely, is subtly different. The irregularities of the wool, the pose of the fingers, the twists of the yarn all differentiate one stitch from the next. But after a few weeks, a few rows, I cannot see the individual stitches in the work. I cannot remember last Tuesday or the day I sat in the sun for hours, just enjoying it. It's all one piece.

P: *Purl.* A backward knit stitch, the purl stitch produces ridges. Some days are purled. They are backward days—twisted. Purls disrupt the flow of the knitting. They distract you from the gentle pattern of the work; they clash; they make a day memorable. A purl day is one full of mistakes. Purls make nothing look right. Sometimes, it seems, one wrong purl can ruin a whole row, a whole section of knitting, throwing off the balance of the work. But, without the purl stitches, the knit side is merely garter stitch.

YO: *Yarnover.* While a yarnover seems to create a stitch, it actually produces a hole. The missing stitch becomes apparent only a few rows later. Yarnovers can be useful in pretending to make up for a lost stitch, but the trick is only temporary; the hole will be painfully apparent in the body of the work. I miss my family, so I watch bad movies on late-night television. Yarnover. I'm struggling in my chemistry class, so I spend more time on my history homework instead. Yarnover. Too many yarnovers in a row, and instead of getting fabric, you get nothing.

YIF: *Yarn in front.* A setup for a variety of complicated stitches. Lavish stitches—twisted, polychromed, multilayered—explode on the fabric, bold and delicate. Cables, bobbles, snowflakes, lace. Friends, straight A's, praise. A hundred small successes. Embellishments that catch the eye; dancing details that highlight the skill of the work and the eye of the knitter. Dazzling, heady, wonderful.

SSK: *Slip, slip, knit.* A slanting stitch used to decrease. Slip, slip, knit saves space and time, but afterwards you have less than you started with. When trying to finish projects, slip, slip, knit is the stitch for completion. There is so much to do, so much work piling up, that I find myself cutting corners and slipping stitches. Words of greeting, a kiss, all the things that count as quality time. Days disappear while I am hidden in a corner of the library, studying. No time for sleeping, for talking, for taking note of the weather. Slip, slip, knit is a stitch best used sparingly.

K (again): *Knitting.* Knitting is the basis, the background. There are mars and mistakes. Elaborate unfurlings and flat repetitions. Patterns and perfection. We wrap ourselves in the fabric. Days unfold, sweaters are finished, scarves are cast on and cast off. Time passes. Knitting doesn't.

Story of Fiber
Wren Ross

I began on the last day of 1991, a noteworthy year. Seven days earlier, on Christmas Eve, I had divorced my husband of ten years. During the process of our separation, a phrase repeated in my head like a mantra: "This fabric is torn beyond repair."

Where does a knitter go to find solace? A yarn factory warehouse, of course. I got into my burgundy Toyota hatchback and sped off down the Mass Pike from Lexington to Uxbridge with visions of fabulous yarns in my head. In the dim light of the cold warehouse, I scrounged through barrel after barrel of gorgeous mohair. I left with a sack that Santa himself would have envied (if Santa knits, that is).

Now I had a New Year's Eve date with some gorgeous hanks. I spread the yarn all over my tiny living room: turquoise, raspberry, purple, green, and lilac—all in various tones. Each color offered so much promise, so many potential relationships. I believe that colors talk to each other. Some are friendlier than others. Blue, green, purple, and rose bonded immediately. I knew that I, too, was beginning a beautiful relationship with this yarn. Through my care and investment, the fiber and I would create something wonderful—but what?

Staring at my yarns, I knew suddenly that I wanted to make a full-length coat of many colors. I wanted this coat to tell the story of the past year: the pain, confusion, and delightful exhilaration of finding new freedom—a new self.

Story sweaters are probably as old as knitting itself. Ever since cave painting, color and shape have served to communicate people's visions of their reality. Think of Turkish socks that tell the story of a courtship. Think of Irish fisherman, identified by their Aran sweaters. Native American blankets that related a good harvest. This coat would be my story of a landmark year.

I began with an overture of stripes. I used the first 4 or 5 inches of ribbing to introduce each color and let them get to know each other. Color is so relative. Put green next to blue and you make one statement. Put purple next to green and a whole different dialogue emerges.

After the ribbing, I considered what to do next. Since everything in my life felt so uneven, I wanted to avoid being ordered and symmetrical. I needed to break free of all constraint. This coat wouldn't just talk; it would ramble. Each panel—left and right front, sleeves, and back—was to be unique. Nothing would match, but everything would go together.

I learned so much from this process. I discovered a new way of listening to myself, following my intuitive impulses in color and design. It was as though the coat was a therapist asking me questions and patiently mirroring my inner meditation.

At first, I used geometry to symbolize what I was thinking. I chose circles to represent a return to my creative life, which had been mostly dormant during my marriage. Squares symbolized boxes: old thought patterns that needed to be opened up. Pink and purple triangles represented my budding relationship with a woman. I moved on to zigzags for the lightning rods of insight I was having in therapy about my relationship to relationships.

Using graph paper, I sketched out Xs to create a motif. Sometimes, I would pore through my large collection of old knitting magazines and books to find interesting shapes, symbols, and designs. I took a great deal of inspiration from the designer Kaffe Fassett, sitting at my crooked wooden kitchen table, sipping tea and thumbing through pages showing his exuberant bounty. I was totally mesmerized.

As the coat progressed, I became more ambitious. I depicted what I loved: sun, moon, stars, and ocean waves. My dear black cat, Molly, graced the front. I put an angel on the shoulder.

But it was my mistakes that proved to be the most honest and revealing. I was starting to feel excited to be single; in my enthusiasm, I decided to knit some tap dancers with hats and canes on the sleeve. Like my marriage, this was a complicated business. When the dancers were done, I noticed that an extra stitch in the design of their feet made them look clubfooted. I left the dancers' feet as I'd knit them because they honestly represented where I was. I was dancing, but it was an awkward and unfamiliar dance.

I learned other things while knitting this coat. I learned that you don't have to follow a pattern to knit. I let myself have a vision, but I let go of any set expectation or goal. No right or wrong—how freeing that was! I was learning to let something be unfettered and full of the spirit of discovery. The project was releasing me from the prison of my inner rules.

I also learned that the process of knitting was important, not the end result. I enjoyed each stitch. What might happen if I applied these new knitting lessons to my life? Maybe, just maybe, I might have a better time!

Looking back, I am amazed how fast I finished my coat. It only took two months, as though my hands were aching to tell my story. I found so much consolation in the colors and truth in the design. The coat helped me to knit myself back together into a person who was more compassionate, accepting, and free.

When I was finished, I made another pilgrimage to Uxbridge, this time to visit Roz. Roz was another knitter, one who was willing to finish my garments, something I was loath to do. Roz lived in a sprawling Victorian house in need of repair. She would sit for hours knitting, smoking, and watching figure skating on TV. She was rough and deeply kind. I was so grateful for her collaboration.

She crocheted buttons of each color: turquoise, lilac,

purple, raspberry, and green. She sewed what I envisioned, making each section of the lining (left/right front, each sleeve, back) from a different brilliant hue of satin coordinated with the yarn colors. The lining looked like a jester's outfit; it would ensure that I wouldn't take myself too seriously.

The Story of Fiber was done. What an accomplishment! I think the beauty of the coat was more than the sum of its parts—its colors and design, the wonderful details of lining and buttons. This coat was to me more than a garment, more than a diary. This coat paid—and pays—tribute to the healing power of art and the enormous comfort of knitting. It says that life does go on even when adversity strikes. This coat had hope and love knit into every stitch.

When I wear my Story of Fiber, I am reminded of my own resilient spirit and how I insisted on making beauty out of a torn fabric. I feel the protection of my own self-love covering me, as though I knit myself a new skin in the process. Finishing it allowed me to start a new chapter of my life—one with more strength, freedom, insight, and compassion, with lots of love and lots and lots more yarn.

Tricoter

Jenny Frost

The first-class compartment was old but well maintained. The red plush seats were firm. Over the back of each bench, a mirror ran from side to side with hooks at each end for hanging outerwear. Overhead, ample metal racks kept possessions out from underfoot and allowed all six seats to be occupied if the train was full. The compartment was comfortable and organized. It felt just as a train heading south from Paris should feel, romantic and timeless.

We were on a whirlwind trip to the Dordogne, the home of rich country pâté and strong local wines. It was a thirty-six-hour odyssey to attend the international publication event for a best-selling novelist's first work in twelve years. We would, in fact, spend far more time traveling to and from our destination than we would actually spend at the place itself.

I was traveling with a colleague, a good-looking man about my own age with whom I was only slightly acquainted. We treated each other with deference, unsure of each other's likes and dislikes but determined to be polite and professional. I did know that he was very much looking forward to the fine wines and substantial meals that the event would surely provide.

The train compartment was not ours alone. At the first stop out of Paris, two older women joined us. They seemed to be about the same age, gray-haired, comfortably dressed in traveling clothes, and carrying shopping bags. I was quite sure they had gone to Paris to visit family and to buy things not available in their local shops. My rusty French was adequate for a friendly "Bonjour!" Then we rode on in silence.

Knitting in front of business associates always makes me feel exposed, vulnerable. How seriously am I going to be taken when I'm holding needles attached to a ball of string? Isn't knitting for fussy old grandmothers? Certainly it's not something a serious businesswoman would engage in—at least not in public. But the train swayed gently back and forth and the movement was irresistible. Four hours in a train, four hours with nothing to busy my hands, four hours just ideal for contented and reflective knitting. The train rolled on, each passing second marking a stitch lost. What a waste it was, I thought, staring alternately at the pages of a book and the scene from the window. And how perfect it would be to feel soft wool flow through my fingers as I knit my way south through France. To gaze out the window at fields and woods and small towns whizzing past and feel the fabric grow beneath my fingers, the train and the knitting forming the best of partnerships—it was too much for me. I succumbed.

I opened my briefcase and with a defiant flourish pulled forth my knitting. My colleague looked over and blinked with surprise to see needles and yarn, not a manuscript, emerge from my bag. My hands quickly found their comfortable position and I sighed with happiness.

"*Vous aimez tricoter?*" The lovely musical French phrase broke my trance.

"*Pardon?*" Rusty linguistic skills, don't fail me now!

"*Vous aimez tricoter?*" the woman sitting across from me in her brown cardigan repeated, with a clear nod at the work in my hands.

"Ah, *oui. Je l'aime beaucoup.*"

With warm smiles, both women opened their own carry-on bags and brought forth needles and yarn. The age and linguistic barriers between us began slowly to crumble under our common passion of knitting. The miles flew by as we discussed our projects and I slowly learned the vocabulary.

We already shared a language, after all. All we needed were the words.

Fables for Knitters

Natalie Harwood, with apologies to Aesop

The Fox and the Grape-Colored Sweater

A fox was walking down the street one day and happened to glance in a store window. He noticed a beautiful, handknit cardigan sweater with silver buttons. He fell in love with the variegated purple yarn and the green cuffs and was determined to have it. He entered the store and asked to see the sweater.

"Sorry," said the storekeeper. "We don't sell to foxes."

The fox went away, muttering to himself, "Forget it. I really wanted a pullover."

Moral: *Purple is not everyone's color.*

The Ant and the Grasshopper

All summer long, the ant was busy storing food for the winter. Then, she sat down and began knitting caps and mittens for her children. She cast on four stitches, knit around and around, pulled the work through at the top, tied it off, and made a tassel. Because she had six legs, she could make three caps at once. Before winter came, she had quite a pile of caps and mittens.

While she was busy knitting, the grasshopper was singing and hopping around in the grass.

"While I appreciate the entertainment," said the ant,

"don't you think you should be knitting something warm for the winter?"

"Oh, sure," said the grasshopper, "but I'll just finish this song first."

So he continued to sing and dance and the ant continued to knit and before long winter came. All the ants put on their caps and mittens and played happily in the snow. The grasshopper, on the other hand, caught a cold and died.

Moral: Plan ahead. Always knit a swatch and check your gauge.

The Country Mouse Knitter and the City Mouse Knitter

Once upon a time, a country mouse was sitting in her plain country mouse hole, knitting with unscoured yarn she had spun herself from wool sheared from her own sheep. Her cousin, a city mouse, was visiting her, and she too was knitting. She had the finest of angora yarns, doubled with a silk thread of shining gold.

"I live in a much finer place," said the city mouse, nibbling on a crumb of wheat bread. "Why don't you come home with me tomorrow? You can have a taste of luxurious living."

So, the next day, they packed up their knitting and went to the city. The city mouse showed her cousin the elegant banquet table, covered with delicacies from all over the world.

While the mice were stuffing their mouths with caviar, lobster, and chocolate Napoleons, suddenly they heard a fierce dog barking.

"Run for your life!" yelled the city mouse. "It's the Spoiler!"

The country mouse was terrified. She grabbed her knitting bag and ran home as fast as she could.

"I'd rather be simple and safe than live in luxury and danger," she said as she fell over her poor country threshold.

Moral: Don't try to knit and cross a city street at the same time.

UFOs: The Lesson of Imperfection

Susan Atkinson

Some years ago, late one night, I saw a UFO. Its shape was amorphous—a black blob dotted with bursts of color, shrouded in a strangely familiar red plastic cloud.

We knitters, even the most resolute, have all seen a UFO: an unfinished object. It is a project that nags at us, calling to us from the back of closets and the bottom of drawers: "Finish what you started." The origins of UFOs are varied. Some projects were too hard; others were too boring. Sometimes we ran out of yarn in the middle, and sometimes we just ran out of steam.

For most of my (self-taught) knitting career, I have stubbornly refused to employ printed patterns. Most of my UFOs therefore tend to fit into the "ill-conceived and doomed from the start" category. Yet these usually experimental works have always taught me much. I have quite a number, but I've never worried about them.

The Susan Duckworth sweater was another matter. By 1988, when this story starts, I had been knitting seriously for about four years. I had finished a few sweaters, even one or two that I actually *wore*.

For Christmas that year, my future mother-in-law gave me

a sumptuous book of Susan Duckworth designs, featuring gorgeous new Rowan yarns. I had never dreamed of such dazzling knitting. Beautifully photographed in luxurious British settings, these sweaters beguiled me. One in particular called out to me, a brilliant sweater called Ellipses.

I have always loved circles, dots, globes, orbs—round objects of any sort. This sweater was covered in circles, knit in a riot of colors. Brimming with overconfidence and enjoying the challenge, I went downtown to choose yarn for this masterpiece. True to my stubborn determination to do it my way, I ruled out any mere yarn kit. Instead, I spent four hours at the Yarn Barn in Lawrence, Kansas, picking out seventeen sportweight yarns to knit this sweater. I vividly recall the salesclerk's strained patience as I kept asking for more help. I spent $110 on the yarn—a record for me at the time. I remember thinking that I would *have* to finish this sweater just to recoup my investment.

Until then, all my sweaters were knit in bulky yarns on size 10 needles. Ellipses was knit on size 2 and 3 needles, at a gauge of 7 stitches to the inch. I had never tried anything so fine. But, fearlessly, I dived right in. I had no idea about intarsia knitting. I knew how to carry a color or two behind, but six or seven?

The first inch was horribly pockmarked and honeycombed and totally unacceptable. Impatiently, I ripped it out and read up on intarsia. I made color charts. I began again. I lost interest fast.

Soon after, I went to China on a grand tour with my new husband. For nine months, we rode the rails all over the Middle Kingdom. Women knit everywhere in China, so I fit right in. I worked on Ellipses in between other projects, slowly beginning to find some satisfaction in the interplay of colors. I began to grasp the weaving-in process of intarsia knitting. I darned endless threads in the couple of pieces I finished.

But it was joyless knitting. My ellipses were all shaped differently, no matter how closely I paid attention. I hated the amateurish look of the work. So I put Ellipses away and finished twenty other sweaters during our two years in Asia.

In 1992, four years after I began, I pulled Ellipses out again. I was unemployed. We had just moved and, like a bad penny, the pieces of the sweater turned up again. The unfinishedness of it bothered me. I watched soap operas and completed a sleeve. But the knitting was still no fun and I put it away.

Every year or so after that, I would come across the unfinished sweater. I always gave the red bag a sidelong glance, quickly moving on to something else. In knitting circles, I spoke of Ellipses in the past tense as the sweater that was, but never would be. I publicly cursed intarsia knitting and became proficient at textured work, even two-handed Fair Isle knitting.

Some sixty sweaters later, the familiar Yarn Barn bag surfaced once more. I was between projects and had no money for new yarn. One evening, I boldly dumped the contents of the bag on the floor and was struck by what beautiful yarns I had chosen more than ten years before. I had forgotten how much of the sweater I had actually completed—both sleeves and most of the front. Looking at the pieces of the sweater, I thought, "This really isn't so bad!" That very evening, I blocked the finished pieces and pinned them together. Admiring my work in the mirror, I said, "This sweater is amazing! I'm going to finish it."

I believe the quest for perfection plagues most knitters.

Knitting a sweater involves a nearly infinite number of variables. Controlling all of those variables is an unachievable goal. Yet the quest spurs many knitters on for a lifetime. Somehow, twelve years later, I was surprised to discover that I was proud of the way Ellipses's mistakes demonstrated my growth as a knitter. The sweater, its errors most visible (of course!) to me, records thousands of miles logged on two continents and years of accumulated wisdom. That night, staring in the mirror, I forgave myself its imperfection.

Six months later, I finally finished Ellipses. I threw myself a party to celebrate, drinking a champagne toast to the glories of imperfection.

Now, if I can just sew on those last two buttons . . .

The Great Unfinishable
Perri Klass

I am not talking about your everyday run-of-the-mill unfinished knitting project here. I have plenty of those—don't we all? I have a pair of gorgeous, if rather oversized, socks, all done—that is, up to the kitchener stitch joining the toe. There was something incomprehensible about those particular instructions, and I put the socks down, meaning to figure out how to join the toes from some other set of instructions—and I just never did. But I will someday. Or there's that elaborate intarsia cardigan I have been knitting for myself for a good ten years. The diagram is kind of hard to follow, and I somehow ran out of interest in the pattern, and every winter I pick it up and add a couple of inches, and I really do believe that eventually it will just finish growing and be done (I mean, I remember when it was just a back; now everything's done except a sleeve and a bit), although, again, it might take me a couple of years to get up the energy for blocking and finishing and decorating. No, my bins are full of projects that I truly believe I'm going back to when the time is right, just as they're full of patterns I'm going to follow before I die and even plastic bags of wool bought with some very particular fantasy in mind.

But even those unstarted projects don't seem as distant and unreachable as my Great Unfinishable. I have come to wonder whether every serious knitter at some point over the years accumulates a project clearly meant to remain ethereally, aspiringly, only partially done.

Mine is a sweater that I started making for my oldest child when he was two and I was an intern training in pediatrics. I made it big, deliberately, as I always do when knitting for kids, both because I think loose clothing is always the way to go with children, and because I want to leave myself a little slack in terms of timing. So, I aimed for a sweater that would be very big on a two-year-old, look fine on a four-year-old, and maybe even live on into kindergarten. That child, who is nineteen, has just finished his first year of college, and he has done it without the sweater.

It was easily the most ambitious project I had attempted. It was a Kaffe Fassett design, row on row of outlined stars. I assembled several dozen yarns in each color category—the centers of the stars, the outlines, the background. I worked with lengths of yarn and makeshift bobbins dangling in all directions and a tattered photocopy of the pattern. I made the whole front of the sweater and it was beautiful. My son admired it, too. He knew it was his star sweater, and he liked me to hold it up against his sturdy little chest to see how far I had gotten.

The problem was—well, the problem could have been so many things. I needed something I could knit in meetings and seminars, and this sweater, with its constant bobbin tending and its ostentatious multicolored complexity, was obviously wrong. Even if I had absorbed the geometric pattern completely and didn't need to check the instructions, even if *I* knew that I was listening to every word that was said, it still looked to everyone else in the room like all my concentration had to be on that intricate, elaborate sweater. It called for comment and admiration, and what I needed was something simple and unobtrusive. And the truth is, even though I had absorbed the geometric pattern, that sweater was pretty busy and my eyes and brain did tend to get caught up in the knitting. *Which color next to which, how many rows to go in the star, how many rows of stars to go in the front, can you believe how beautiful this is, can you believe I am creating such a thing?* And then, on top of that, I stopped feeling comfortable bringing the sweater out of the house with me at all. So many hours of work had gone into it, so many decisions, so many damn bobbins: What if it were lost or stolen? What if one of my colleagues got pizza on it at the next noon conference?

It did occur to me that all of these same considerations would apply to the sweater itself, if I finished it and put it on my child. But I don't really think that any of this was rational. Nothing was going to happen to the sweater at work—nothing ever happened to any of the other projects I dragged through the hospital. If I had completed it, I would have put it on my son and it would have withstood the various spills and scrimmages of childhood. No: I think that what happened to me with that sweater was that I came up against my Great Unfinishable, the project which, for complex reasons involving my temperament, the shape of my life, my beliefs, and my destiny, was always meant to remain in progress.

I think about the story—I don't know whether it's true, but it's certainly told often enough—that master Oriental rug makers always deliberately include one mistake because nothing made by human hands is supposed to be absolutely flawless. I wonder if in the life of a knitter—or of certain knitters—there needs to be a project that will always exist as something attempted but not fully attained, a thing of beauty that is not yet a thing of use. All I can tell you is that, unlike those untoed socks, which periodically nag at me, I seem to be at peace with the star sweater in its partial state. I think it's beautiful. I pull it out and look it over every now and then and marvel at it, but I don't think seriously that it's getting to be time to pick it up again.

Sometimes an unfinished project signals something wrong, something pathological, something stifled in a life; consider the would-be writer who struggles with a never-to-be-finished novel that somehow blocks all other possible projects. And some famous unfinished artistic projects were overtaken by death or fate or history. Consider Leonardo's bronze horse, which he had to abandon in 1499 when the French attacked Milan; the Italians used the bronze to make weapons, and the French, after taking over the city, destroyed the clay model by using it for target practice. But there are also plenty of famous Leonardo projects that were left unfinished by the artist:

drawings for paintings he never painted, paintings he started but didn't complete. We tend to see those as evidence of his fervent, teeming creativity. (Not that I'm suggesting any comparisons to me and my star sweater!)

The child for whom the star sweater was started now wears mostly T-shirts with in-joke slogans and jeans from the Gap. In fact, my youngest child is now, at eight, too big to wear the sweater. But somehow I don't feel like I missed my chance, or like I let something precious go to waste. Instead, I think that sweater supplied beauty and aspiration and mental exercise and a vast rainbow of color back at a time I needed it. I think that taking it on and learning to follow the instructions led me much further than I had ever been into the intricacies of complicated knitting. With every other project with ambitious colorwork that I have ever contemplated, a reassuring voice in my head has pointed out that next to the star sweater, this would be simple. I treasure what I actually created, and what I dreamed of creating; I treasure my own ambition, and my willingness to push against the limitations of my skill and the realities of my daily life.

But will I ever get to treasure that sweater, complete in all its glory? Ever get to see it worn by some important child or other? Some far-off unimaginable niece or nephew or (dare I even say it) grandchild? To be honest, right now I don't think in terms of relearning that geometric pattern and sorting out those bobbins and dangling ends; I have a long and at times onerous to-do list where knitting projects are concerned, and I regularly ignore it and buy new yarn for some new scintillating darling that has caught my eye. The star sweater is nowhere on my list at all.

But maybe one of the joys of a Great Unfinishable is the distant tantalizing possibility that I will change, or that life will change, or the heavens will shift into the right configuration. I do keep the half-made sweater in a bag, together with all the different balls of yarn involved in its making. I know the pattern is in the Kaffe Fassett book on my shelf. Perhaps, someday, I will be a different knitter, a different person, a woman who might actually finish that sweater. Perhaps, I will surprise myself. The chance to do just that is part of what I treasure in that plastic bag—that bag full of many many different colored yarns and rows of brilliant stars.

Villanelle for Anthony
Jamie McNeely

Anthony sits in his overstuffed chair,
knitting endless scarves until they are done.
In the middle of night, no one knows he is there.

He casts on stitches with silence and care,
a stitch for each year of his life: forty-one.
Anthony leans in his favorite chair,

whips through black cashmere, raw silk and mohair,
the fabric unraveling like a dog's tongue.
In the middle of night, no one knows he is there.

His sisters said, "How many scarves can we wear?"
each Christmas, as soon as the night's begun.
But Anthony sits in his broken-down chair

and knits whether they notice or care,
whether they laugh or whether they shun,
whether they even know Anthony's there.

Clouds to the east and a chill in the air.
He always insists that he does it for fun:
Anthony knits in his comfortable chair.
In the middle of night, no one knows he is there.

Creator/Creating/Creative: Knitting the Spirit

A Psalm

Donna Jaffe

I knit stitches into sweaters
  God knits people and deeds into a world.
I create designs in yarn.
  God creates designs in people and deeds.
I unravel my mistakes to repair them.
  God lets mistakes play out so we can mend them.
My creations serve me and my loved ones.
  God's creations serve God.
I bless my loved ones with my creations.
  I praise God with my creations.

God has blessed me with creativity.
God blesses my loved ones through me.

Prayer Shawls
Carole Ann Camp

There they sit on the table in a pile, a temptation for any kitten looking for a good time: balls of yarn. Subdued greens and blues, the color of healing waters; browns and tans and golds, Mother Earth shades; and the joyful reds, oranges, and yellows of fire and compassion—each waiting its particular calling. They'll make no ordinary hat or sweater today, but instead a sacred gift.

The clock ticks toward four. The door opens, and Agnes, closing in on ninety-three, pushes her walker toward the table. Hands barely able to hold the needles any longer, she struggles into her chair, rummages in her knitting bag—a gift from a grandchild nearly fifty years ago. She finds her size 10½ needles and looks at the yarns before her. Eyes on the yarn, she slips into a waking dream, drifting through years of knitting baby booties, sweaters, socks, mittens—so many mittens, more than anyone could probably ever count.

The door bangs open, jolting Agnes out of her reverie. Jamie, dressed (or nearly dressed) in teenage black with violent dark lipstick and wires jutting out from her nose, ears, and lips, plunks herself down in a seat and starts to poke at the yarn, squeezing here and fondling there.

More women arrive: Alice and Martha, both retired; Edna, another elder pushing a walker; Emily, with one twin toddler holding on to each hand and a baby strapped on her back.

The school bus pulls up in front of the church. On Tuesdays, the bus detours from its normal route to let ten-year-old Meghan off here instead of at home. Still shy about her knitting, she finds a chair in the circle of women gathered around the table. Hoping not to make too many mistakes, she casts a longing glance toward the soft dark purple yarn. Agnes had told her last week that the nubbly yarn was harder to knit but showed fewer mistakes. Maybe she'd try that one today.

"Where's Peter?" Alice asks. As she speaks, the door opens to a tall man, about fifty, with thinning red hair. "Speak of the devil!" Martha giggles.

"Who are the prayer shawls going to this week?" Meghan wants to know.

Edna rustles in her knitting bag for a slip of paper. "Here's the list. Sarah is in Beth Israel Hospital in Boston. She's thirty-one and has a six-month-old baby. She had a slight cold, but it turned to Guillain-Barré syndrome. It's lucky she went to the doctor's when she did. Her prognosis is good, but she'll be in the hospital for a few more weeks.

"Next, there's Janice, who's ninety and in the nursing home. Her son died in December and just this past week her daughter died, too. She is grieving. It is so hard to lose both of your children.

"Third shawl. This last week, Catherine's X-ray showed more cancer. She's no longer in remission. She also learned on Monday that her mother has breast cancer. The rest of this week's shawls will go to the women's shelter."

Emily speaks up. "I'd like to knit a prayer shawl for my friend Becka who just discovered that she's having twins this summer. I know how much I appreciated the prayer shawl you knit for me when I was pregnant." Her eyes fill with tears at the memory.

"Good, let's get started then."

"Let us offer a prayer before we begin," Peter suggests. "I call forth nine blessings from above, in the name of God, the Creator, the Giver of Life, the Holder of Time; in the name of Jesus, the Savior, the Healer, and the Lifter of Pain; in the name of the Spirit, the Comforter, the Consoler, and the Sustainer of Life. Amen."

Emily takes some water-blue yarn for Becka, thinking of the waters protecting her friend's unborn babies.

For Catherine, Edna chooses earth tones. Meghan takes deep purple for one of the women in the shelter. Peter, Jamie, and Alice also decide to knit for the shelter. Martha holds out warm gold for Sarah, while Agnes starts in with white for Janice, who has been her friend for almost seventy years. As the knitting begins, the knitters chant prayers around the circle. The prayer circle turns, rises into the air, becomes a mantra of healing. Prayer gets woven into stitch after stitch, row after row.

"I knit a mantle of caring."
"I knit a mantle of protection."
"I knit a mantle of wholeness."
"I knit a mantle of strength."
"I knit a mantle of healing."
"I knit a mantle of patience."
"I knit a mantle to enfold you."

"I knit a mantle to encircle you."
"I knit a mantle to empower you."

Rows become inches, inches become feet. The prayers of healing flow on into and throughout the yarn.

As the knitting draws to a close for this day, the knitters pass their work around the circle for a final blessing.

In the beginning, creating God, you formed my being.
You knit me together in my mother's womb.
To my flesh and blood you gave the breath of life.
O loving one, renew me this day in your love.
Grant me life as gift of your faithfulness;
Grant me light to journey by;
Grant me hope to sustain me.

May this mantle be a sign of your healing presence.
May it warm Sarah, Janice, Catherine, Becka, and all the
    women in the shelter when they are weary;
May it surround them with ease when they are suffering;
May it encircle them with caring when they are in pain.

May your gentle yet strong touch reach out to heal all the
broken and hurting people and places in our world. Amen.

[adapted from "A Prayer for Healing" by Cathleen Murtha, d.w.]

Sweater Grace

Claudia Conner

That sweater turned up again the other day. Over the years, I have thrown it under the bed, onto the floor of the closet, into the backs of drawers—anywhere so I wouldn't have to look at it again. I should have thrown it away. I wanted to throw it away. I wanted—but I couldn't. Every time I looked at it, it was just such a nice piece of work. The knitting was intricate, time-consuming, attention-getting; and no matter how I abused it, the sweater never got dirty. But it made me angry every time I looked at it, every time I thought about it, so angry that I couldn't speak.

I started the sweater several years ago on a Christmas trip to Oregon. It was a pattern I had been wanting to make for a couple of decades—complicated knitting, difficult to plan out and hard to describe: mirror-image cables made up of double twisted-stitch lines, twisted-stitch ribbing, horseshoe cables, and an intricate, twisted-stitch, diamond-shaped center panel 35 stitches wide on both front and back. I changed the pattern to make it saddle-shouldered, knitting the horseshoe cable in bands out to the side from the neck ribbing, hanging the front and back from the bands and the neck ribbing, and then carrying the horseshoe cable down the sleeves with the mirror-image twisted-stitch cables on either side. I knit the body in the round, from the bottom up, with no seams, rethinking the center panel and cables so they could be worked on the front of the garment instead of knitting back and forth, front and back. When I got to the yoke, I went back to knitting back and forth, front and back. It took about two months of concentrated attention to make, a long time for an expert knitter (and after nearly thirty years, I thought I might be something of an expert).

I don't own a knitting pattern book that does not say in clear, bald, bold-faced English: **Make a gauge swatch.** I didn't do a gauge swatch. I picked a size from the pattern that I thought should do it, and started right in.

After about 2 inches, I realized I had a huge sweater in process. Instead of taking it out and starting over, I decreased gradually at the sides, getting everything down to where I wanted it by the time I got to the yoke. I knit the saddle shoulder onto the front and back yokes, and then the sleeves out from the body, and finally the neck ribbing, weaving in the yarn ends. I put the sweater on.

It was triangular. The bottom belled out absurdly. I wore it a couple of times and then began to think about how I might alter it to fit better. If I had had a sewing machine, I could have stitched two lines straight up each side to catch all the yarn and then cut it open row by row and woven the ends in. But I didn't have a sewing machine.

So I took the sweater across the street to the cleaners and asked the woman there to have the tailor sew seams in double lines straight up the sides. Just that. Nothing more. She smiled broadly and nodded yes a thousand times.

Now, I know from working with refugee programs that when people whose grasp of English is weak smile broadly and nod vigorously, it often means they have no idea what you are talking about and they wish you would go away and leave them alone. But I ignored my experience (when have we ever done anything *with* our better judgment?) and put my sweater into her hands.

I went back the next week, but she said, "Not ready." I went back a week later and she said, "Not ready." I went back a week later and she said, "Ready." I paid the five dollars and took the sweater home.

When I unfolded it, I couldn't believe my eyes. The tailor had cut the sweater apart from hem to sleeve cuff. It now had a straight seam up the side and down the underarm. The sweater was no longer a triangle. When I put it on, it fit well.

But the tailor had done the work on the *right* side of the sweater, not the wrong side. The seams were heavily overcast, making large, flat flanges standing up on the outside of the body and sleeve. It was unwearable.

I couldn't bring myself to take it back to the cleaners. I remembered how hard I had pretended that the woman had known what I was talking about. It was my own fault that the sweater was ruined. I stuffed it away.

It turned up again the next year. It turns up every year. I can't get rid of it and I can't get away from it.

It turned up again last Saturday. I sat looking at it and thinking again that I should throw it away. Then, I had an idea. Maybe I could knit the flange into submission with I-cord. I found the leftover yarn from the sweater and sat down to try. It didn't work. The flange was huge; no I-cord could cover it without looking truly idiotic. I looked at it again. Maybe I could crochet it down. I tried. But the flange was solid with sewing thread and wavy—wider at some points, narrower at others—and still stood out from the side. I looked at it some more. Then, it came to me. I would sew it down with yarn. I got a yarn needle and did it. It was easy. You can hardly even see that there's a flange. You can feel it with your hands, but it's not uncomfortable when you are wearing it. I put the sweater on the next morning to go to church and gratefully accepted compliments such as, "Did you make it yourself?"

I have always said that knitting is a forgiving craft. You can make any number of little mistakes that won't really show. But this sweater has taught me that I never knew what forgiveness really means, neither in knitting nor in life.

I always thought that if you did something bad, and you felt sorry that you did it, you could make a sincere apology or amends or atonement, and you could/would be forgiven. I never realized that the something bad might in fact involve a terrible wound, an awful scarring; something that made a big ugly flange in a life that would have to be stitched down into a big welt that would never go away. That welt might be invisible to the eye, but always there to the touch. I never realized that forgiveness might have to mean accepting an irreparable harm in order to forgive and heal the person who caused the harm.

The sweater does look pretty nice on me. It has forgiven me. But it and I will always know how my carelessness and impatience and hardness of heart hurt it. Its forgiveness of me makes me want to cry. Who knew there could be so much grace in such a thing?

Still: If only that sweater would also forgive a certain thickness around my middle, I am sure I would look even better in it.

The Sock Heel
Molly Wolf

(for Jane, my sister)

Dammit.

Dammit. Dammit. Dammit. Dammit. Dammit.

I slipped my knitting off the needle and yanked out rows until I got back to the stitch I'd dropped. I find it best to pick up stitch loops by running a piece of fine string through them with a blunt sewing needle, so that they can't unravel as I pick them up. So I did that, resettled the work on its double-pointed needle, and got back to working back and forth across the heel flap.

I like knitting socks. This is a Big Knitting Secret: Socks are fun. They're small enough to go fairly quickly; they tend to be playful and even a bit kinky; and above all, they're magic. There's that bit at the bottom where you turn the heel, a highly mysterious and (at first) incomprehensible business of knitting, decreasing, turning, purling, decreasing, turning, knitting—and, out of what seems like complete nonsense, there emerges a beautifully sneaky bit of 3-D fabric construction. Socks are *clever*. And they make you aware of generations of knitters before you who have gradually added to the store of cleverness now emerging from your needles. Socks sum up a particular type of quietly important cultural evolution, more neatly than most things I can think of.

As long as you knit them right, that is. . . .

I'm making these socks for my sister. Her taste in clothing tends to run the gamut from well-bred beige to subtle gray, with the occasional hint of subdued green or blue. Myself, I feel that her wardrobe needs cheering up. So I found this magical yarn, dyed so that it knits itself up into stripes with no active intervention on my part, and I found it in a deliciously fruity mixture of wild sherbet-y pastels, and I have added some matching hot pink for the tops, heels, and toes. The result is—well, lively. Yes, definitely. Yum.

The first sock went just fine, except for a little fogginess on my part about the toe decreases, but it all looks quite normal and nobody will ever know. But, for some reason, when I got to the heel flap of sock number two, I started to make mistakes. I have now taken the damned thing off the needles five times to rip out rows and reknit—a process that knitters call "frogging."

You frog a piece of knitting when you've made a mistake that you can't gloss over or go on with; you've got to go back and fix it. Neophyte knitters hate to frog, because it looks like such an ungodly waste of time—all that work ripped out . . . More-experienced knitters know that frogging is as much a part of knitting as is purling. Frogging is simply inevitable, human nature being what it is.

I've become comfortable with—even accomplished at—frogging. I rip my knitting off the needle without a backward glance and reach for that needle and length of string, thinking, *I just wish I could do the same for nonfibrous matters.*

Unfortunately, while knitting can run backward, unraveling to a particular point, lives can't. We make decisions knowing that they're irreversible, knowing that they may be mistaken, but that they must be made nonetheless. I had to do one of those last week, reversing a previous choice that had turned out all wrong.

But making a choice and then reversing it is not the same as frogging. It's more like adding a stitch to make up for the one you dropped. The two errors don't really cancel each other out, any more than two wrongs make a right. You may end up with the same number of stitches, but the flaw remains. Each choice has its consequences that have to play themselves out in time.

My two choices don't eliminate the consequences; they elaborate them, complicate them, like the pattern of ripples made by dropping two pebbles into a puddle, one next to the other. But the choices still had to be made, for better or for worse—and we never know at the time. I can't frog those decisions, merely live with them.

Psychiatry thought for years that it could frog the human psyche—that its practitioners could unravel a soul back to the errors that had scarred it and set them fully to rights. But life doesn't work that way, either. We may understand the past and forgive it—forgive it truly and deeply—but it still leaves its marks on us. In that sense, we may be healed, but we are never cured.

There is no possibility of slipping our lives off the needle and yanking time out to go back to where it went wrong and set it to rights. Not in this life, at least. Our time runs one-way—the gift of the Fall, the angel standing at Eden's gate with a flaming sword.

I wonder sometimes if, after death, God frogs us—holds us firm, undoes the years of pain and wrong and suffering, reknits us together in eternity's womb, so that we emerge in glory, just as we should have been if this life weren't so broken and bloody imperfect. And, maybe, for some of the souls I know— some who suffered such horrible damage so early that they've wandered through life, heroically coping with unimaginable pain—God will do just that.

But I don't know. These socks for my sister are not as finely knit as perfect machine-made socks would be; they can't be. They're coarser in weave than bought socks, visibly hand-made. Even superb sock-knitters like my mother-in-law turn out socks that are clearly handmade. But isn't that the whole point? There's no love in a mass-produced sock. There is deep love for my sister in each stitch of these silly, imperfect socks. Maybe after death, instead of frogging us, God simply trans-forms us, until the love in us swamps the errors and we emerge perfect, transformed.

Or, as Grampa Simpson says, a little from column A, a lit-tle from column B. Who knows? We'll find out when we get there.

There. Heel flap done at last, heel turned, stitches picked up to unite heel with sock body, gusset completed; we're on to the foot now, racing for the toe. This is plain straight knitting, round and round, the sort of knitting I can do while watching TV or listening to the radio. It's quiet work, but satisfying. The end is in sight.

Jane, you'd better wear these. And *in public*, you hear? No cheating.

Binding Off

Janis Leona

When my daughter Kate was sixteen, she went to a boarding school in Sedona, Arizona. That year, when she came home to northern Minnesota for Christmas, she brought her boyfriend, Adam, home with her. Also a student at her school and from Phoenix, Adam had never played in snow before. He spent hours building snow forts with Kate's five-year-old sister Chloe. He stayed outside so long, I worried about his digits. That summer, Adam came again. He swam in the Schoolcraft River with the same childlike exuberance he had shown in winter.

Back at school that fall, he was withdrawn. Then, with some vague reference to "having to find out who I am" and "needing space," he abruptly left school, dumped my daughter, and joined (or so she heard) the Hari Krishnas. Annihilation was total. Adam was the love of Kate's young life— literally, her first love. This is the boy for whom she had sneaked out of her dorm late at night, just so they could lie on their backs together on the red rocks surrounding the school and gaze up at the stars. This was the one person she could stay awake all night talking to and be able to say anything. He was her best friend, her first lover, closer than a brother—her mirror self. Her soulmate.

Five years passed. Kate was twenty-one now, and in a committed relationship for two and a half years. She had never heard from Adam. Sometimes, she would dream of him and wonder if he were still alive.

In early December, on Chloe's eleventh birthday, Kate looked at me across the dinner table at an Italian restaurant and asked, "Do you remember teaching Adam to knit that Christmas he visited?"

I did not—I remembered few details from that time. But I certainly remembered the spirit of the time that Adam spent with us. It was pure love and innocence.

"Don't you remember?" Kate pressed on. "He drove us all nuts back at school with his knitting. He knit between classes. He knit during classes. He knit on hikes. He had this nasty, blue, fifty-foot thing wafting out behind him. He dragged it everywhere because you never taught him how to bind off. Mom, you never taught him how to *stop knitting*."

After Kate reminded me of Adam's knitting, I couldn't stop thinking about him. I had forgotten that I even knew how to knit. Suddenly, I began to knit obsessively. Before, I had always abandoned any knitting project before completion, not having the patience to finish, but by Christmas, just three weeks after hearing that story, I had twenty scarves to give to friends and family—people whom I love. Then a weirder thing happened: I began to knit scarves for people I didn't even like, for those with whom I had unresolved issues, for "difficult" people. What was even weirder was that every stitch healed something in my heart I still cannot name. I began to feel love for those people, too.

All the while, I kept having this image of Adam sitting on the edge of a huge, orange crescent moon, his long dark hair billowing about him, knitting stars into that same nasty blue scarf. Adam, boy in space, still knitting—unable to stop knitting—for the Hari Krishnas. I started to see Adam everywhere: in the twinkling eye of the freckle-faced redhaired young man behind the counter at the gas station; in the dark, dreadlocked singer in the front row of a local high school boys' choir "Sweetheart Serenade" concert the week before Valentine's Day; in the soulful gaze of our funky-looking little dog, Maisie, whose tongue always hangs out the right side of her mouth.

Adam was in Kate's thoughts constantly, as well—and in her dreams. After five years, she was still angry, sometimes bitterly. She was still in pain. There had been no resolution for her. Even though she is happy in her current relationship, she has not forgotten what she'd had with Adam. There was razor wire wrapped around her heart, and if his name came up, or a mention of the Hari Krishnas, or anything else that reminded her of Adam, the pain was swift and sure.

Then he called.

The night before Valentine's Day, Adam called from Phoenix, where he is alive and well and going to college. He didn't say who he was. He didn't have to; she knew immediately. His first words after five years were, "Kate, I'm so sorry. I was such a dickhead." It turns out he was never with the Hari Krishnas. He had been traveling all over the world for five years working with his own Roman Catholic church—a revision of fact which completely blew away my Hari Krishna/knitting/space-boy image.

What Adam said next is an image that will stay with me for the rest of this lifetime and perhaps beyond. He said that when he had been with Kate back at school, it was as though he was holding a whole sack full of gold, and then he saw a pearl off in the distance on the peak of a mountain and he dropped the gold and went after the pearl. "All I did," he said, "for five years was to struggle to get almost to the mountaintop, only to slip and fall back to the bottom, again and again."

What he realized after he stopped struggling was that he already had all that he had been searching for. It was love. It was that same thing that he'd had with Kate. And that there was not a second during the past five years that Kate had not been with him. Finally, he had "found himself," and who he is is love.

As Kate told me what Adam had said, we both started to cry. Kate, for what she once perceived as her loss—of Adam, of her innocence, and for her battered young ego. Me, for the beauty of Adam's self-discovery: that we all already have everything we need, all the time, right where we are. We do not have to search for it. We do not have to go off on some solitary quest to find it. We do not have to work at it. And we cannot lose it. We have access to it anywhere, anytime we stop struggling. And, if we can remember to live from that place, "the issues" do not matter. What matters is relationship. What matters is unity, or integrity.

Perhaps this is what every stitch knit in all those scarves was about—uniting my heart and mind so I could fully understand the unimportance of issues, details, or circumstances, and recognize the holiness of relationship.

Stash
part three

IN WHICH WE PLAY WITH YARN IN MANY FORMS, FROM
SHEEP TO SHAWL, IN DYEING AND SPINNING, IN ODD
BALLS THAT DELIGHT US IN THEIR SINGLENESS.

Odd Balls: Bits from the Stash

Editors' note: Some pieces defy categorization. They are like the odd balls in stash, none the less precious because they don't match any others. That's why we've called these pieces "odd balls."

BEEPBEEPBEEP
Barbara Wagner

Aigh.

I roll over and somehow manage to switch off my alarm, all the while wondering why I'm willing to get up at 4:15 on a Saturday morning so I can go sit in the cold and the wet for hours. Oh, yes. There's the race. Not that I ever really forgot. I sit up and switch on the light. All I can manage after that is to sit and blink at the walls of my room.

BEEPBEEPBEEP.

Damn. The snooze is still on. I reach over and prod my clock again.

I get up and stumble across my room in the approximate direction of my sports bag. I grope around inside, squinting. I get dressed, body and brain still complaining. All I can think is *Thank God spandex is comfortable.*

This is a good thing, since I'm basically wearing nothing but. I ought to say now what the clothing of a rower in late fall is comprised of; it's rather interesting, at least to one who wears it regularly. Over the usual socks and underwear goes the "Uni," aka "one of those bathing suits with legs." Made entirely of spandex—in my case, navy bottom, scarlet top with a white stripe down each side—it does really look as though someone had gotten extremely drunk one day and sewn a pair of biker's shorts to a swimsuit. Not the most stylish piece of clothing ever designed. Not too flattering, either. Especially on guys—well, I'm sure you can figure out for yourselves why they tend to find the suit a bit embarrassing. Next comes a JL (or two). Also made of spandex, it's a very, er, formfitting long-sleeved shirt. Also in the team's colors (obscenely bright scarlet, white stripe down the arm, WINSOR in navy down the left arm). Then the usual long spandex pants, sometimes sweatpants, several sweaters, headbands, hats, and, finally, the famous Winsor "waterproof" jacket— waterproof, that is, until water actually touches it. Then it becomes instant wrong-way Gore-Tex, wicking the moisture into the rest of your clothes, while keeping sweat from evaporating into the environment. Good for the environment, maybe. Personally, when I'm wet and cold (as we often are), I couldn't care less about the environment. I'm too busy swearing at the jacket.

Why have I taken so much time explaining the race-day clothing of a rower, you ask? Well, clothing is probably the one thing keeping us alive when our coaches have us out. It's I-don't-know-how-many-degrees-below zero, the other team's coach has just swamped us, it's snowing, and, even after we dock, we have to slosh through puddles of icy water for at least fifteen minutes. Once, the puddles inside the heated boathouse froze, it was so cold.

Socks are a rower's best friends. I mean it. Especially the nice, dry socks you always have in your bag, because you are a smart rower. I am, and I offer you proof. I have my toes, and they are attached to my feet. Everyone who forgets extra socks doesn't have any toes anymore. Just kidding. They really just mooch socks off of others. Once a pair of my socks made a round of the entire team last year before finally coming home to my bag, and they weren't even handknit.

By now, I am dressed in so much clothing that I'm having trouble moving. I go look for breakfast. It's five o'clock; I hear my father stirring.

Fast-forward.

"Alexis, where the *hell* are you?" our frantic coxswain (henceforward "cox") is shouting into a cell phone. It's now around six-thirty and I've got a sudden burst of hyper energy. I'm bouncing around the parking lot, receiving death glares from most of the others. Laura goes on shouting, demanding that Alexis get here *right now* or we'll miss the race. I can only imagine what Alexis is saying, but I'm pretty sure that whatever it is, it contains a high percentage of Bad Words. Every obscene word I know I learned from sitting in front of that girl for two seasons. Goodness, that was a shock, freshman spring.

Fast-forward. Somewhere in New England.

My bag is wedged against me. A tussle ensues as I attempt to yank out a Ziploc bag with my knitting in it. I have a pair of my best friends, socks, in the works. (Green socks from that really cool kind of wool which makes a design all by itself.) Alice throws me a weird look—I've started singing under my breath without realizing. The weather looks unpleasant. I knit, looking forward to warm feet some time in the foggy future. Reagan is driving, talking to her friend Cindy, who (if we believe Cindy) was dragged along on this trip against her will. I drift into complete calm as I knit, fingers flying, watching the road, my teammates, and the top of Reagan's brilliantly red head moving slightly as she drives and tells us stories.

Fast-forward. Somewhere in Connecticut.

It's cold and drizzly. I'm sitting under a tarp rigged to a couple of trees and the trailer to keep the rain off of our bags. I've finished one sock, and some of the team are staring at me in fascination. You'd think I was showing them a waterproof raincoat. So far, I've explained the pattern yarn six times, and people are still watching in apparent awe. Many have asked me to knit them socks. Alexis even offers to pay for a hand-knit pair.

As usual, nobody is quite sure about what's happening, so everyone but the rowers is running around, trying to figure out what's next—coxes going off to their meeting, coaches talking to other coaches. The rest of us just try to keep dry. I feel the chaos flowing around me, but I am held outside those flows of nervous energy by my knitting. I am bound to the earth like a rock in a riverbed, bound by the twined yarn in my hands, rhythmic movement creating a music which is almost spell-like. I sit outside of time, as gradually everyone else goes to sit in the vans, driven inside by the cold and the damp. Now I sit, alone under my tarp, and the rhythm of my quiet work falls in the silence. Even though we are right up against the trailer and boats of another crew, they are separated from us more surely than if there were a 10-foot wall. I float in silence, and my work holds me there, quieting the nervousness I would normally feel, keeping me in a soft, safe void. My work holds me there, until I am drawn out by my cox's call to run the warm-up. I am ready to race again.

Fast-forward. After the race, heading home.

I don't remember what happened during the actual race—I rarely remember even the cloudiness I feel when there is too little blood in my head because it's all going to my muscles, pulling, concentrating on each stroke, one after the other. I don't remember what Laura said to us to drive us over the—what? 3 miles?—of river. Or what place we came in. It doesn't matter in the end.

What does matter is the rightness of doing what you're supposed to do—not in the sense of obedience, but more "this is what I've been taught, this is what feels right, this is where I belong, this is what I'm going to do." I remember I sat on the water in my Uni and JL in the rain and cold for an hour-and-a-half before racing, freezing while waiting to do something painful and exhausting, watching steam rise from my body. Strange how this should feel right. But it does.

As it does when, hours later, I'm sitting in the van going home, and I knit until my eyes are blurred with sheer exhaustion and the light is gone. I'm in front with Lisa, another coach, who tells me to watch the boats on the trailer to make sure they don't slip. I fall asleep against the window, mind swirling through the darkness and rain, soft bag cradled on my lap.

I would live like this forever if I could, traveling with the rough, rowdy, bad-mouthed, loving mixture of coxes, rowers, and coaches, in a corner of the world both brutal and kind, knitting warm socks for all those who row through the cold and the rain, to return to the warmth of the boathouse and its familiarity. Maybe one day I'll be able to knit for all those who share the corner of society I've found myself in. I certainly have no desire to leave.

Not-Cleaning
Suzanne Cody

My daughter is napping. I am writing. What I would normally be doing while my daughter is napping is knitting, but today I am writing about knitting and that will have to do.

What I am *not* doing, however, is cleaning.

At this particular moment, there are dust rhinos (bigger than bunnies and more vicious) setting up housekeeping under my chairs and behind my bookshelves. Small toys lurk in the cracks of the couch cushions. There are dirty dishes in the sink, as well as a lovely skein of yarn I recently dyed with grape and cherry Kool-Aid.

There are colored markers and bits of paper all over the unvacuumed carpet, along with a shoebox, some tissue, and a hand-drawn card, detritus of my daughter's aborted art projects from maybe three days ago. The bathrooms—well, we just won't talk about the bathrooms. I can say I have cleaned both of them thoroughly sometime in the past month. I'm not sure when, exactly, but I believe it was right around the time I was knitting a fluffy purple mohair pullover for a pregnant friend.

The stairs need sweeping. The laundry needs folding and putting away. The beds need making. My kitchen floor—well, you know about Superfund sites? It could be one of them.

Everything is covered with a very fine layer of dust.

There are four knit placemats and one coordinating napkin sitting on the dining room table waiting for their companion three napkins. There is an unfinished pale green mohair cabled cardigan in a knitting basket. A gray wool all-over-cable scarf languishes in a knitting bag hanging from the handlebars of my daughter's tricycle—which is, incidentally, parked in the living room. There are mittens in various stages of completion in various spots around the house. Although I find it convenient to pick up a project to work on in any spot I happen to be not-cleaning in, I have to admit that my unfinished projects do add to the chaos.

Nonetheless, I am not cleaning. I am not cleaning because I am writing. I am writing about knitting in lieu of knitting, which is what I would normally be doing when my daughter is sleeping. At the age of four, she can make knitting while she is awake a challenge. Writing about knitting is the only thing I can imagine doing if I am not knitting. Or taking care of my daughter.

The dust rhinos will still be there tomorrow. Or next month. Or when my daughter is grown. They are peaceful now. Why bother them, when I could be knitting?

The Visit

Michael Learmond

Four boys sat uncomfortably in the front room. Each was washed, scrubbed, combed, and warned of the consequences of misbehavior. Mother was polishing the teacups. Father was tinkering with his new knitting machine in the other room. All were waiting. Waiting for "the lady."

The card had arrived a week ago, fluttering onto the mat without a hint of the frenzy of cleaning and tidying that it would induce. It had announced that, since my father was now the proud (and discerning) owner of a Knitwizard Elite 4610 (pat. pending) multifunction knitting machine, a fully trained expert demonstrator would visit him in the comfort of his home, in order to explain the operation of the machine. My brother Robert had earned a red ear from Mother for suggesting that obviously no one from the manufacturers had ever visited our street before.

So it was that the family waited, in the summer of 1969, for Miss Carol Hemphill to show us the ropes (or perhaps, as Robert suggested, "to spin us a yarn").

When the doorbell finally rang, we four children giggled as if directly wired to the bell by the front door. Robert whispered, "Take your seats, please. The show is about to begin!" Mother stood up, straightened her skirt, glowered at Robert (although I swear to this day, I saw a twinkle in her eye), and went to answer the door.

Poor Miss Hemphill. You see, we knew, and she didn't, that our father could make any knitting machine do pretty much whatever he wanted. He was to a knitting machine what Rembrandt was to a canvas, what Beethoven was to a piano, what Georgie Best was to a football. The only person in our family who didn't know this was Dad himself.

Dad had only bought the machine as a way of earning some extra cash in the evening. He worked with what he called the "infernal machines" every day, had done since he was fourteen. He grew up in the Scottish Borders, where knitwear was quite literally a way of life, as it was one of the very few ways to earn a decent living. He had been trained by masters of the art. In turn, he'd been sent here to Ireland, to help set up a new factory and (as Robert put it) "to teach the natives how to knit."

At last, Mother showed Miss Hemphill in. She was a quiet blond young woman with a rather tense smile and a faint air of awkwardness. She was also wearing the most horrendous bright yellow knit suit I had ever set eyes on.

"Can you sing, Miss?" enquired Robert, sweet as you like.

Miss Hemphill looked a little startled, then obviously decided that our Robert was a bit simple. "You must call me Carol. And no, I can't sing very well." She smiled nervously at Mother. "Goodness, the questions they ask!"

Robert went in for the kill. "Oh, Miss . . . sorry . . . Carol. It's just that I thought all canaries sang beautifully." He drew his eyes up and down the yellow suit. As Carol colored with embarrassment he added quietly, "Red and yellow go so well together, don't you think?"

Carol turned to Mother in confusion. "This suit is a wonderful example of what can be achieved using the Knitwizard

Elite 4610. With a little practice, your husband could soon be producing garments of similar quality."

Mother appraised the suit. "I'll take you in to see Jim," she said in the tone of voice she normally reserved for dealing with itinerants and sundry unsavory characters. The two of them moved toward the rear room to the background noise of "Cheep, cheep. Carol the canary," from the younger family members.

Dad stood up as the door opened. "Ah, you must be Miss Hemphill. I'm Jim." He smiled a greeting.

"Please, call me Carol. Oh. I see you have managed to get everything set up already. To be honest, some people have found the handbook a little difficult."

Dad looked puzzled. "Handbook?"

"Oh, come now, Jim. I can see where your son gets it from. I've already been caught once already tonight. Now, shall we get on?"

Dad shrugged his shoulders. "Certainly. What tricks and tips can you show me?"

At last, Carol looked a little more confident as she felt herself moving into familiar territory and about to take control. She sat down beside my father on the vacant stool by the machine. "Well, I like to say, 'Let's learn the trade before we try and learn the tricks of the trade!'" She smiled patronizingly. "Firstly, I'll show you how to thread the wool through the machine and how to produce a simple knitted cloth. You'll be amazed how quickly you can pick it up."

Dad said sheepishly, "Actually, I've already had a little play on the machine. I hope you don't mind."

"Don't be silly, Jim," replied Carol. "After all, it's your machine. Would you like to show me what you have made?"

She added, "Please don't be embarrassed. I'm sure I've seen worse first attempts."

Dad reached behind the chair and retrieved the sweater he had made the first night after he had assembled his machine. He reached it to Carol, still folded.

"Thank you, Jim. This looks really very good." Carol stood up in order to let the sweater unfold. Her smile froze, then faded as she stared at the front of the garment. Dad had used more than a dozen different colors of yarn to produce a stunning bird of paradise as a design. The effect was breathtaking. He had used tiny lengths of emerald green wool to color the eyes. The wings were flecked with gold and silver. The bird was set against a background of a shimmering oasis.

Carol regained her composure. "I'm not sure what sort of a game you are playing here, but surely you didn't expect me to believe that this was produced on this machine? It's simply not possible. I should know because I know this machine inside out and I am expert on its capabilities."

Dad knew that he would not win the argument by dialogue. So he did what he did best. Carol watched, bemused, as Dad's fingers flew across the needles gently tweaking and teasing the yarn, checking and adjusting the tension every few moments, every stitch produced with unerring perfection.

One hour later, a bewildered Carol took her leave, clutching a present from my father. It was a new knit suit that demonstrated the capabilities of the Knitwizard Elite 4610 knitting machine.

The only trouble, Robert quipped, was that her employers would never believe it.

Weinhardt

Nancy Huebotter

It all started with a plea from a co-worker: "My dog, Weinhardt, gets so cold, and I've never been able to find a sweater to fit him. Do you think you could knit him one?" Sandy explained that this dog had scarcely enough hair to keep him warm. She had seen my prize-winning sweaters—the ones I'd made for my niece and nephew—and she knew I was an accomplished knitter. She was sure I could create a sweater for her four-legged family member.

I didn't know much about Sandy's dog except that he was almost like a child, coddled by my friend and her husband. Providing the little pooch with a means of keeping warm seemed like something I could do. How difficult could it be? The pattern should be simple enough. I knew my grandma had whipped out sweaters for her chihuahua. Sizing up my own miniature dachshund, Liesl, I decided I could do the same.

Since my grandmother had died some years earlier, I'd have to find other resources to consult about my project. I couldn't contain my amusement when I called my favorite crafts store, asking if they had a pattern book with instructions for a dog sweater. I was sure Nana had created Cisco's sweaters by pure trial and error, but I needed a definite pattern. The knitting consultant at the Best Little Knit House has no doubt had numerous strange requests for patterns, but I was sure this one ranked among the strangest. However, Mrs. Purkey took the request seriously and managed to find a book. She'd keep it for me until I could stop by.

The pattern looked simple enough. Mrs. Purkey was sure that, with my knitting expertise, I would have no problems making a sweater for that sweet little creature, a garment that would keep him warm while ensuring that the dog would be making a fabulous fashion statement.

Feeling like a clothing designer, I armed myself with the pattern book and a tape measure, and then drove to my friend's home to meet my canine customer. In response to my knock, a deep-throated bark reverberated through the door. What the hell was that?

The question had barely registered when Sandy opened the door and the most massive Great Dane I had ever seen bounded out to greet me. My initial take told me that the animal's head was bigger than my whole diminutive Liesl. What had I gotten myself into?

Weinhardt, properly introduced, eyed me up and down. With much trepidation, I let him sniff the back of my hand and my shoes. I was surprised by his gentleness as he rubbed his head against my hip—a sign of acceptance, I assumed. Cautiously, I petted his huge head and said a few friendly words, as much to reassure myself as the dog.

Formalities between dog and designer over, the dog's owner commanded him to lie down on his blanket. Going by his response, he must have graduated summa cum laude from obedience academy. As Weinhardt folded his massive body onto his bedding, he snatched up an infant-sized teddy bear, then cuddled it as gently as a mother cuddles her child. Even so, I was a bit uneasy as I started taking his measurements. Clearly this was going to be a much bigger project than I'd expected.

No way did Weinhardt's measurements match any sweater pattern for the largest dog listed in the instruction book. I thought of calling Mrs. Purkey and asking her if she had any patterns for a Shetland pony. Probably not.

Making the pattern workable would require calculatory wizardry well beyond my mathematical abilities. Thanks to a friend with an analytical mind and a multifunction engineering calculator with advanced math capabilities, we came up with an algorithm that calculated the difference between the measurements given in the instructions and Weinhardt's. Then we could extrapolate the ratio and determine the number of stitches needed to fit the Great Dane.

The one skein of yarn I had purchased would, however, clearly be not enough.

With all the confidence of a professional knitter, I cast on and began. It was a simple stockinette stitch with periodic increases and decreases for fit. I attacked my project with proficiency, gradually forming the neck, then the body, of the sweater. As the sweater grew and took shape, I needed to schedule a fitting, to ensure the proper placement of the upper-leg openings. The dog greeted me with a friendly wag of the tail. Patiently, he let me lay the garment around his upper body and calculate how many rows I needed before beginning the leg bands.

A few weeks later, I had worked the garment to the desired length. We needed another fitting before I could begin the next step. Once again, Weinhardt was cooperative. No doubt about it, our relationship was growing—a kind of mutual trust cradled in caution. After all, pound for pound, we were comparable in size. He was stronger; I was smarter. He had teeth; I had knitting needles.

A few more weeks, and I had the sweater almost finished. Weinhardt would be getting his custom-made garment before the winter months. It would provide him with the ultimate in collar-to-tail cold-weather protection.

Anxious to show Sandy, I stuffed the doggy clothing into a bag and took it to work. I was holding the sweater up against my 5-foot-3 frame when a group of engineers strolled by. One of them viewed the outfit with interest—it stretched from just under my chin to my ankles. He noted casually that I must have misread the instructions; the armholes for my dress weren't in the right place.

After taking up nearly seven skeins, I'd finished Weinhardt's sweater. I had just enough yarn left to knit a small sweater for my Liesl. The measuring and calculating exercises were the same, but the knitting itself took mere days.

Now that the sweaters were finished, we planned to get the two sweater-wearing dogs together for a photo session—the photos would be priceless. But, one day, when Weinhardt was on his appointed rounds of the neighborhood with Sandy a few strides behind him, a moppy little mongrel brazenly gave the big dog a piece of his mind. Obviously, the small dog was jealous of Weinhardt's sweater. Weinhardt responded by picking up the little dog by the nape of its neck, much as he would his teddy bear, and carrying off the terrified creature. Shocked by this out-of-character performance of her gentle Great Dane, Sandy reined in her animal and Weinhardt released his hold on the frightened pooch. After that, I called off the photo session; I was too worried that Weinhardt would do the same thing to my Liesl.

I was sure Liesl would love her doggy knitwear since she regularly burrowed beneath her bedding blankets. But it was plain from her demeanor that she thought an extra layer completely unnecessary. She uttered doggy complaints about being forced to wear "that thing." She would endure the garment briefly, and then slink off to the bedroom, where she ducked under the bed and wriggled out of the hated encumbrance, emerging later, clearly proud of the fact she had outsmarted me.

Weinhardt wore his sweater with pride. After all, he was the best-dressed dog in the neighborhood. I'd made his sweater in worsted-weight yarn, tan with muted flecks of color. Its suggestion of tweediness made him look as though he'd come from the moors of England.

Without a doubt, Weinhardt equated me with his new-found comfort. I don't think it was just the familiarity we'd gained during those ridiculous fittings. Somehow the big guy knew that our friendship was knit of something more than yarn and mutual respect. The audible sigh and the love and gratitude in his doggy eyes when I slipped the finished sweater on him said it all.

The Perfect Plan

Adrienne Martini

Forget Richard Simmons. Goodbye, "miracle" products. Farewell, Dr. Atkins's low-carb. Rather than rely on the so-called experts, I decided to devise my own custom-tailored weight-loss program.

On paper, the two-pronged fat-attack plan was foolproof.

Prong one emerged from my box of knitting shame, which was overflowing with uncompleted orphans crying for some attention. Every time the cookies in the kitchen whispered my name, I would pick up a knitting project and complete a couple of rows, hoping that small diversion would dull the sirenlike cry of sweets. In addition, knitting must burn a calorie or two, moving me just one small step closer to achieving prong two, which was to get more exercise.

It should have been a win-win for all involved. I would be a step ahead this Christmas and have plenty of items to bestow on family. A friend's baby would receive his sweater in record time, long before the first cool breezes of autumn started to gust. And I would lose a few of my own postbaby pounds. Once my middle decreased just a smidge, I would fit back into a bunny-soft cashmere sweater I'd begun long before getting pregnant. The promise of a new, snuggly top for the winter might be just the motivation I needed to finish the second sleeve and actually put the thing together.

My plans often serve better as cautionary tales than inspirational stories. And this one was no exception.

The whole exercise thing disintegrated a day or two into my weight-loss program. The daily, somewhat sleep-deprived struggle to get everyone up and fed, bathed and dressed, left me ready for another few hours of sleep rather than a brisk round of calisthenics. Nice long walks do happen, but only when the stars align, the moon is in the seventh house, and I am able to find both of my sneakers in less than twenty minutes. Gone are my thrice-weekly tennis games, replaced with nothing more strenuous than rolling around on the floor with a baby who squeals delightfully. The trade is more than worth it.

Knitting instead of snacking has been somewhat less of a failure. Busy hands make unwrapping mini Snickers bars difficult, while caramel-covered fingers make for messy projects. After a few days, my two-pronged scheme couldn't be called a rousing success, but it at least showed potential.

I had not, however, factored in the devious nature of yarn designers.

One night, while I worked away on the baby sweater and studiously avoided thinking about the ice cream in the freezer, the names of the wool I was using sprung unbidden to my mind. Bisque. Sweet Potato. Cocoa. Suddenly I wasn't knitting a nice earth-toned garment; I was crafting a meal. I drooled with each sweet potato stripe, dreaming of a cream-and-butter-filled casserole topped with brown sugar and pecans. Each beige round called up my husband's crab bisque, a rich concoction of corn, red pepper, and seafood. Cocoa led my mind inevitably to chocolate—a rich, bittersweet torte, perhaps, or a sinful mousse.

Knitting wasn't taking my mind off food anymore; it was only adding fuel to the flames. My fiery imagination needed a cooldown. It needed ice cream.

Did I need to put my projects on a diet as well? Could I only allow myself diet-friendly yarns like celery, lettuce, and beet? Did my yarn stash need to be purged of any skein named after a food with more than 30 percent of calories from fat? Or had treat-deprivation led me to hallucinate?

It was a knot that I couldn't quite manage to untangle. But rather than put away this tiny, yummy cardigan, I decided to revel in it. Just because I shouldn't dive mouthfirst into a big bowl of hot, sweet cocoa, my fingers shouldn't be denied the pleasure of handling such satisfying yarn. Matter over mind, I reminded myself, and forged ahead, adding one delicious stitch after another.

With each stitch, I dreamed of luscious knitting projects: a tam in crême brûlée with caramel stripes and a mixed-berry tassel; an eggplant parmesan jacket with tomato and basil polka dots; a pair of mocha milkshake socks with cream at the toes. My appetite could be rechanneled, it seemed, and any drool removed in the wash.

Oddly enough, this bit of mental trickery worked. The sweater for my friend's baby is three-quarters complete, lacking only a sleeve and the final assembly. And while no one will ever mistake my behind for J. Lo's, my fiber-filled hands have been less likely to dip into between-meal treats. It's not a perfect system, granted, and I wouldn't make millions if I marketed it—although given some of the stuff that brings in wads of the green stuff, I do wonder if I shouldn't give an infomercial producer a call. But it seems to be working about as well as expected.

As an added bonus, my next several gifts are already planned and each has roots in my culinary urges. No one else need know why my knitting tastes have started to run toward the edible.

Now, if some spinning genius could just come up with some hot fudge sundae–scented yarn . . .

Learning to Knit at Fifty
Christine Lavin

I spent the first fifty years of my life not knitting. I was busy doing lots of other things, but knitting wasn't one of them. So why, at fifty, did I start?

I live in New York City. One theory why so many women here have taken up knitting recently is that it's a kind of post-9/11 hands-on stress reliever. Could be. Immediately following 9/11, I went on a baking binge, kneading so many loaves of bread that my hands got swollen. So I cut back and paced myself. I discovered that baking bread helped to keep me sane when I was home. It also made me popular with my neighbors, the local firehouse, the laundromat, dry cleaners—even a local restaurant, although the pastry chef was alarmed that someone was dropping off loaves of *petit pain au chocolat* for free. (But that's another story.)

My work—I am a touring singer/songwriter—takes me on the road, where baking bread every time I get the urge isn't possible. Hotel kitchens don't allow it. Believe me; I have asked.

I didn't realize I was looking for something else to do on the road until early September 2002, when New York was in the throes of dealing with the first anniversary of 9/11. I saw a news report on NY1, the local all-news station, that a yarn shop in Manhattan, the Yarn Company, had been overrun with New York women who had a sudden desire to knit. As soon as I saw that report, I knew I was one of them. I called the Yarn Company and signed up for a three-hour group class. The deal with the Yarn Company is that you take one class—that's all you need to get started—and then you can come in for the rest of your life and they will help you with your projects. It's a policy they should probably rethink, based just on me.

At 7 P.M. on October 1, I joined a group of three other beginners. We were taught how to knit and purl; then we were told to pick out our yarn, decide what our first project would be, and begin. Our teacher strongly urged the first project be a sweater since scarves are boring and too easy to really learn anything about knitting. I'm proud to say that I am the only one in my class who took that advice. I chose a practical yarn, an oatmeal wool. I knitted a swatch and had my measurements taken. The teacher printed up a pattern and cast 72 stitches on circular size 11 needles. At 10 P.M. she sent me on my way.

Four hours later, at 2 A.M., I was desperately surfing the Internet, using the Google search engine in my vain attempt to learn how to make a slipknot. I had completely goofed up my first row of knitting and tore everything out to start over. But I didn't know how to make a slipknot, and without that, casting on was impossible. I looked at Boy Scout web sites, fishing web sites—but at 4 A.M. I turned off the computer and, disgusted with my ineptness, went to bed.

The next day I was back at the Yarn Company. An instructor there recast the 72 stitches and I sat for hours working on those first difficult rows. Slow going. The next day I came back, sat there, and knit for hours more under watchful eyes. Already, spontaneous buttonholes had begun to appear in my sweater when I worked at home by myself. An instructor at the Yarn Company told me to rip out and redo the rows with the holes. I was shocked at the thought. "This is my first sweater," I told her. "Everything I do after this will be much better. I want to see where I started from." The truth was I simply couldn't face the idea of ripping out what had taken me so many hours to knit.

My concert work took me on the road that weekend to Colorado. Hearing that airlines were strict about certain carry-on items, I switched from metal needles to bamboo for the flight. When I landed I switched back to metal. An hour before my show in Fort Collins, I had a brainstorm. I brought my knitting out onstage with me, and just before intermission asked if there were any knitters in the crowd. Could they add a few rows to my sweater to help me with this first project?

A man—yes, a man—did exactly that during the intermission. I thanked him from the stage and he proudly announced to all of us that it was easy for him; he was an advanced knitter. "When my wife and I took a Lamaze class before the birth of our first child, I knitted a uterus for the teacher!" The crowd fell silent. Too much information. The next night, in Denver, I asked for intermission help again, and at the end of the concert, my sweater was four rows longer.

I came back to New York City and, on October 8, went to an event at Madison Square Garden, a benefit concert for the family of Timothy White, the editor of *Billboard* magazine, who had died. Some of the artists on the bill weren't of much interest to me, and so I decided to knit during those sets. Hey, I'd been knitting for eight days now; surely I was experienced enough to knit in the dark? Not. The ball of yarn fell to the floor and when the lights came up for a break, two men from my row dashed out to beat the crowd for the beer line. They ran between me and that ball of yarn. Within thirty seconds, fifty people were cursing and yelling at me as I chased down the wool and tried to untangle them. Embarrassed as I was, I secretly congratulated myself on choosing oatmeal, a shade that doesn't show dirt.

When I got back to my seat, two teenage girls behind me said loudly, "What kind of a person comes to a rock concert and *knits*????" I pretended not to hear them.

The lights went down. The next performer was James Taylor—I loooove James Taylor, so I gave him my full attention. For about thirty seconds. I thought, *Hey, wouldn't it be great to get James Taylor's vibes into my first sweater!* So I took out the yarn and continued knitting, but this time making sure the ball of wool didn't travel. I knit two rows during James's act. When the lights came up I was dismayed to see two very visible mistakes in what I had just knit. But I didn't tear those mistakes out, either. They are my James Taylor spontaneous buttonholes.

Later that month, I working in Boston, and on an off night I went to see Dame Edna (my all-time favorite performer) at the Colonial Theater. Barry Humphries (Dame Edna's alter ego) gave me a complimentary ticket in the fourth row. While waiting for the show to begin, I knit two rows. During intermission, I knit one more. Now not only did I have James Taylor in my sweater, I had Dame Edna, too.

I decided to bring that first sweater to every musical or theatrical event that I could, to get all those good vibes into the knitting. When I finished it, I wore it to a concert in Bellmore, Long Island. I showed Jay, the sound man, the various mistakes throughout (there are more on the back, the first part I knit, than on the front or the sleeves, so I already could see that I was making progress). I said to him, "The funny thing about mistakes in knitting is that you have no idea you are making them till you come around again. You have no memory of doing something wrong. They somehow spontaneously appear. That's why I call them spontaneous buttonholes."

"But they're not spontaneous buttonholes," he said. "They're crop circles."

Works for me.

From Sheep to Shawl
(or, Baa, Humbug)

Hot Wire!

Rosanne Anderson

A few years ago, when I first started raising a small spinning flock, I found that creating the perfect sheep-proof fence was a full-time occupation. When I felt like I'd tried just about all possible combinations, I hit upon the idea of outlining my pasture with a strand or two of electric wire—hot wire. I figured that a hot-wired fence about nose-high would keep the fluffy critters in, and I'd add a higher strand to keep the larger livestock out.

Because I had so few, my sheep were pretty docile, more like pets than real livestock. They would indeed live out their lives with me—just as long as I could keep them fenced. They liked to follow me around, creating problems when I tried to move from place to place, but they kept our barn and building areas mowed and weed free. I kept them penned on a small bluff behind our house, which was perfect for sheep. They seemed to enjoy keeping it mowed, and I didn't have to worry about doing the job myself.

One day, trying to ensure that the sheep kept out of the adjacent horse pasture and in where the little darlings were supposed to be, I was walking along the outside of the fence, checking it and talking to the flock, when suddenly something scared William, my white Columbian. Sheep panic easily, you know; anything can set them off—the sound of grass growing, a cloud passing by. Of course, panicky William ran straight at me, his Person, to save him.

The hot wire didn't even slow him down. His head was up; there was no way for his nose to come in contact with the hot wire. Nothing was going to stop him. Nope! He charged right through the fence, breaking it, tangling it, and dragging it straight toward me.

I saw the danger as William trailed the still-hot wiring behind him, and yelled at my beloved husband (who was down below, watching the drama unfold), "Shut off the power!" I distinctly remember shouting this several times in a variety of versions, but all he would say as he ambled toward the general vicinity of the switch was, "What? What'd you say?" But I heard his laughter as I skipped and zigged through the brush, out of poor William's terrified way.

I don't have William anymore; he lived out his life in luxury and safety, especially after I changed all of the fencing. No more hot wire for me. There are not enough *helpful* people in times of need. Good old cattle panels and field fence will do just fine.

The Uneasy Fiber Source
Micki Smith

"Work 'em, Plunkett!" That was my novice command to my six-month-old untrained Australian shepherd. They were out again, those silly sheep —a motley flock of ancient breeds, with fleeces only a mother and inveterate knitter could love.

Plunkett's highly pedigreed genes run deep and he instinctively began darting, bobbing, and dropping into an intimidating crouch. Even my two excited young granddaughters couldn't distract him.

Sheep, on the other hand, are infinitely distractable. At first they couldn't decide which was the greater threat: screeching, hopping, pint-sized humans or the dog with the big white teeth. But they soon recognized Plunkett's innate authority and he herded them neatly through the sturdy wooden gate, which I quickly latched behind them. Plunkett's tailless hindquarters rotated excitedly and he looked at me saying (in dog terms), "Wow, Mom, look at me! Didn't I do a great job, huh, Mom? Huh? Huh?"

The sheep at our Vermont country inn are a new enterprise. A knitter since early childhood (taught by a loving grandmother), I'd recently taken up spinning. Visions of handspun, handknit sweaters danced in my head. For spinning, you need fleece; for fleece, you need sheep. Jumping into this fledgling endeavor with both feet, a soft heart, and no knowledge whatsoever, I'd bought these unwanted refugees from three different flocks. Margot and Joan were twin Tunis. Max, named after a gruff former boss, was a wethered, four-horned Jacob. Schaf (German for "sheep") was the aggressive black Shetland ram lamb, purchased to service the ewes, eventually.

But, very soon, reality struck. This was work. Smelly, costly work. Worst of all was the issue of containment. No matter how hard we worked to keep fences intact, the sheep—particularly horned, efficient Max—managed to escape. While meandering sheep provided entertainment for our guests, they bode poorly for gardens and left great piles of pellets for unsuspecting feet. Thus Plunkett.

All went well for the better part of a year. Schaf matured and hormones enhanced his masculine proclivities. That Shetland respected only one thing: Plunkett. Whenever I had to deal with Schaf, Plunkett was by my side. (There's a reason for the name *ram*!) One day, the sheep had made yet another escape and Plunkett was summoned to duty. Plunkett, crouched and stalking, zeroed in on Schaf. Schaf, head lowered, huge curved horns glistening in the noon sun, fixed his unblinking gaze on Plunkett. The dog sniffed the air as if some new scent had caught his attention. He sniffed again and crept closer to the ram. The black head bent, nose to earth, his hooves dug into mown turf. Plunkett inched forward, still sniffing. I hovered, close by but sufficiently safe, hoping for at the very least a standoff. Suddenly, Plunkett stuck his nose forward into Schaf's left ear and began licking. Every virile muscle of that ram relaxed. Plunkett licked. The ram lay down and turned his right ear. Plunkett kept licking. The other sheep stood transfixed and I laughed uncontrollably.

My laughter was short-lived, however. This little breach in Plunkett's authority widened fast. Anarchy reigned. More accurately, Schaf and Max took control.

Spring shearing brought the situation to a head—mine! The experienced shearer handled the ewes efficiently and sent them naked into the chilly March air. Max grew more agitated with each swipe of the electric shears across Schaf's body. He snorted and stomped in protest of his fellow ram's indignity. I leaned languidly, arms akimbo, on the wooden gate watching this age-old procedure. Sweater patterns swirled in my head: a subtle cable for my grandson, a seed stitch to show off Margot's coppery sheen . . . Without a warning, without so much as a bleat, Max hunkered and sprang, clearing the gate but not my head. (Jacobs are known for their ability to leap 6 feet up from a standing position.) His curled front horn caught me on my left eyebrow, smashing my spectacles and knocking me back into the muddy barnyard muck. Blood mixed with wet dung as the shearer pulled me up, talking me back into consciousness. Plunkett hovered sympathetically, fearing to leave my side to chase the errant Max.

Enough! These guys were going to market. Face washed, peroxide applied; fleeces skirted and tucked into pillow cases, I bade the shearer farewell. He probably laughed all the way over the mountain. The slaughter's truck arrived the next day, hauling two reluctant male sheep to their destiny.

We communicated the departure of Max and Schaf to our granddaughters, who mourned appropriately for three- and six-year-olds. "What will you do with their fur?" the littlest asked.

"I want a hat, a Max hat," added the older.

Nursing my petulance, I put off preparing the fleece for another full season. Periodic prodding from the granddaughters finally moved me to wash and card the wool. The batts sat in my storage cabinet for another year before I took up the project again.

Max is now spun, his three-colored coat melded into a soft gray, nubbly yarn. It's time to pick up some size 5 double-points, ease into the rocker in front of the fireplace, and cast on the proper number of stitches while Plunkett snoozes at my feet.

What Do You Do with a Dead Sheep?

Laurie Clark

I look up from my knitting to watch the snow dance outside the window. A winter day, snow falling, my knitting at hand—magic. Balls of wool like the tops of ice cream cones sit in my tapestry bag, waiting to become scarves, socks, and mittens. This wool is special. It doesn't come from a yarn store or mail-order catalogue. No, this yarn is far, far dearer.

A few years back, my love of knitting took several new twists and turns, and I began to explore other fiber arts. Intrigued by the ways in which strands of twisted fiber could be transformed into an intricately structured web, I turned my focus to weaving. In time, the mystery of warp and weft pulled me in yet another direction. Spinning became my passion. With a cloud of Corriedale fiber in hand and stocking feet on the treadles, I watched fascinated as bits of fluff turned into fine yarn. Was my fiber curiosity finally satisfied?

That question got its inevitable answer the next spring. "I need sheep," I said to myself.

You must understand that fiber arts aren't my only passion. I am a pet person. If it has feathers, fur, a shell, or scales, no doubt it lives in my house. It would come as no surprise if hoofed animals would eventually join the family, but where would they live? My city backyard obviously wouldn't do.

I called my friend Christine, also a spinner, and told her of my idea. She was game to take up sheep farming. Residence was no problem; my sheep could live with her in the country. She would play parent during the week and I would visit on the weekends, a mutually agreeable custody arrangement.

And so, our experiment in sheep husbandry began with three lambs, Percy, Clancy, and Toby. Naively, our heads danced with dreams of mountains of fleece—glorious fleece, the bounty of our three new pets—spun into skeins of soft yarn. We didn't know a thing about wormings, inoculations, manure, or worse.

The call came in the early evening: Percy was sick. Christine had called the vet. The diagnosis was plant poisoning. In nature, don't most animals tend to know what they should and should not eat? True, in general. But sheep are not of that intellectual caliber.

Christine met me in the driveway and quickly related a story of thunder, panicky sheep, escape, ingested mountain laurel, an obviously sick sheep, and a frantic call to the vet.

We syringed white goo down Percy's throat with a plastic turkey baster, no easy job with an uncooperative sick sheep. We laid him, sad and pathetic, on a bed of clean hay for the night.

"He seems to be doing much better," Christine called to tell me early the next morning. Relieved, I went to work feeling confident that the crisis had passed. I would visit after work.

That afternoon, I found Toby and Clancy contentedly munching hay in the pasture, but no Percy. I checked the pen—empty. I feared the worst. On my way to the house, I discovered a large lump lying covered with an old quilt at the far end of the porch. Percy was dead, eyes cloudy, bits of stomach-pumping residue still clinging to his mouth. I stood there for several minutes feeling terrible and helpless.

Sitting down on the steps, I contemplated the problem: What *do* you do with a dead sheep? You can't bury it in a small box like a hamster or flush it down the toilet like a goldfish. As I sat and mused over our predicament, Christine arrived. We talked quietly about the vet's desperate efforts and our own sorrow. Then, silently, we stood together on the porch staring down at Percy.

After a few minutes of quiet contemplation, I thought the unthinkable. Was I being morbid or simply practical? Our eyes met.

"I'll get the shears," was all Christine said.

Shearing a dead sheep is certainly easier than shearing a live one.

We gently wrapped Percy back in the quilt, only head and hooves protruding, and wondered how we would ever dig a big enough hole in which to bury him. Christine headed for the phone. Within minutes, the rumble of heavy machinery reverberated down the street, and a neighbor turned his large yellow backhoe into the driveway. Our burial problem was solved.

Percy now rests beneath the grass behind the sheep pen, his feet angled to resemble a sheep gamboling in the field. But he is still with us. We washed, dyed, carded, and spun his wool into soft, luxurious skeins of pastel-colored yarns.

Now on a snowy day, I turn back to my knitting. Needles settle comfortably in my hands and the magic resumes. Percy's fleece eventually will warm necks on frosty winter mornings, protect feet from chilly rubber boots, and, best of all, protect granddaughters' little hands from the bite of winter's cold.

That's what you do with a dead sheep.

Fiber Addiction
Donna Nothe-Choiniere

Perhaps I could blame it on genetics, or on being born two and a half weeks late, but I prefer to look at it as something very much my own, something I am proud to own . . . I think. Fiber addiction: a chosen condition.

My mother taught home economics; she had worked for *Vogue* and similar publications before she married my father, who worked at a woolen mill in town. They both had fiber in their blood and they spun it off to me. That's the genetic link. As for my delayed birth, it explains why I'm always behind in my spinning.

I always wanted to own sheep, and once I learned to spin, I wanted them even more. I would look at cats and long-haired dogs with fiber lust—would muskrat hair make nice mittens? Could the guard hairs of road-killed porcupines be spun into something useful—say, a horse harness or a dog leash? The leash would be for a border collie, of course. A border collie would be great with the flock of sheep I really *needed* to have.

We seldom socialize, since my tiara has been at the jewelers' for years—it needed cleaning, you know. But when we do go out, I note that at public social functions, people have a way of coagulating into distinct clumps. It's not hard to read the dynamics. Guys talking sports to the left; women with children under ten talking child care and teachers' competence to the right. Lawn afflictions, please stand next to political enthusiasts. Stock players, brokers, money managers, form up near the side door, please. Long-lost chums, center field; "my wife dragged me here," together with "my husband dragged me here," close to the lost pals; frustrated women who haven't had a date since Clinton left office, circulate throughout. There: room mapped. Me, I'm looking for the folk who farm or have animals. We want room to ourselves to talk about sheep and llamas and what the hay's looking like this year.

You greet others of your kind with comments like "We're Romneys, mainly, but we're looking for a good ram with long wool, good crimp, on the fine side—not necessarily in breed, however . . ." "Oh! Please say hello to the Cheviots." "Did you see the Dorsets coming in?" "Did you know he's thinking about converting to Lincolns, but if she has anything to do with it, it'll be Jacobs—she's a Jacobs kind of gal." "Yoo-hoo, here he is, Mr. Hampshire! First prize at the Big E!" It can get pretty outlandish. Soccer moms shy away, repelled, when they hear "Yup, I had a slovenly day. Had to help Mary elastrate tails this morning." The point (whatever it was) of the social gathering fades into insignificance as we get into the really meaningful stuff—well, meaningful to us, anyway.

I suppose driving 10 or 20 miles out of your way to look at a flock could look a bit pathetic. Leaping into your truck and tearing off to the other side of the county when you hear that So-and-So has a new ram, just for the chance to get a good look at the ovine studmuffin and judge his probable performance with the ewes, might seem a tad obsessive. But there it is.

When you're a real fiber addict, shopping is a problem. Clothes come in sizes and textures and colors and shapes, but not in specific yarns. You see a sweater that catches your fancy, and you have to pick it apart, mentally if not literally. It's 100 percent wool—great! But *which* wool? The sales help are useless

"Excuse me, miss? Do you know anything about this sweater?"

"It's a size ten, real trendy this year—"

"No, about the fiber?"

"It's 100 percent wool . . ."

"And—?" you prompt gently.

"It's green—and it's *made in the U.S.A.!*" She grins like a third-grader coming out with the right answer in a spelling bee.

"But who made it? Where did the wool come from?"

She's getting uneasy. "I dunno, a sheep or a goat or

something—you'll have to ask the manufacturer." And she scurries away.

Pathetic! You study the label. Cheviot or Lincoln . . . it says Shetland, but is it *pure* Shetland? It smells and feels more like a blend. Doesn't seem to be carbonized, but that smell—definitely wool and sizing, maybe a hint of fabric softener. You rub the sleeve on your chin and look for a stray fiber to tease out. A micron count would be nice, if that better microscope that your husband ordered for his job comes in. You're sniffing the sweater again and trying to pick at a loose spot, when the salesclerk gives you that look and picks up the phone to call her boss. Time to check out the linen department. Did anyone say pima cotton?

I find myself reading historical fiction, looking for references to spinning. Weaving gets mentioned once or twice, but not nearly often enough. Romance novels, no. That Texas vixen might be doing something with her mare's mane and tail hairs, but she'd rather be in bed with the handsome rancher or staunching his bullet wounds. Hmmph. Plenty of sex, but no spinning. Boring. But then I hit pay dirt. I'm reading Anita Diamant's *The Red Tent*, and if that doesn't make you want to bake a batch of hard bread and get out your drop spindle, you are not with the program.

Rabbits. The fiberholic must have bunnies to stay sane. We have eight Angoras and one drop-off who thinks he's Angora. You make excuses so you can stay home and pluck. Paid work is nice because it keeps you in sheep food and bunny chow, but the Real Thing is feeling aboriginal angora coming off into your fingers, into your yarn. You dream of hats with halos. Far more rewarding than unrewarding customers—unless, of course, they raise llamas or alpaca. . . .

Are you a fiberholic? Here's a simple test. If you can answer "yes" to all or most of these questions, you're one of us. (If you have one or more "no"s or "maybe"s, see me.)

1. Is one or more rooms in your house insulated with wool?
2. Do you collect sheep shears, sheep print fabrics or buttons, porcelain llamas/rabbits/camels, or other fiber-animal collectibles?
3. Does a picture of a musk ox or a flock of sheep hang above your fireplace?
4. Are you interested in the Peary or Shackleton polar expeditions solely because they both depended on wool and silk to get them through?
5. Do you look at old cotton mattresses as a potential source for interesting spinning?
6. Have you ever bought Mylar because it could be chopped up and unraveled to provide glitter to incorporate into your own yarn?
7. Do you ever scan a field of weeds with an eye for dye plants?
8. If someone says "milkweed" or "yucca" or "cedar," do you immediately think of fiber?
9. When weeding around the woad in your garden, do you find yourself screaming, "Grow, baby, *grow!*"
10. Have you ever bought one or more bookcases specifically for your spinning / weaving / dye / knitting / sheep / angora / camelid / felting books?

It has been said that you cannot be a little bit pregnant. Either you have fiber in your blood and lanolin under your cuticles, or you do not. If you do, you will not be a ninety-day wonder, falling in love because spinning looks so romantic; you will not be a five-year-planner, who will move on to stained glass, which you will later ditch for pottery or rug hooking. No; you will be among the few, the dedicated, the people I brake for: those who wear lanolin like perfume, those who are looking for ways to turn goat-hair grease into soap, those who move to a different state where the dye plants are better. These are my soulmates.

If we are to be separated (as the Bible says) into the sheep and the goats, I want to talk to God about the quality of the flock. Which breeds? Are they horned? Do they twin every year? What's the pasturage like? How much wool per animal? Are the goats bossy Nubians or Angoras? God, send me some fine black Angora goat hair and I'll make a robe for Moses or Benjamin or maybe even Jesus. . . . Amen.

The Stuff of the Matter: Wool

Mariah Educates the Sensitive
Susan Blackwell Ramsey

In the first place,
you are not allergic to wool.
That lie is the bastard brat
of ignorance, overheating, and vanity.
You may be allergic to cats,
Angora rabbits,
dust, mold, pollen, the stings of bees,
bad dreams, the semen
of Rh-negative men,
or, if you were an axe murderer
in a former existence,

strawberries. You could be reacting
to chemical dyes, the sulfuric acid
they soak wool in to carbonize the hay,
sheep dip so deeply lethal
it kills on contact, bad vibes
from an old cryptorchid ram, hysteria,
or bad karma. But not wool.
Never wool.
Has it ever crossed your mind
that there are breeds,
that each breed extrudes
a different wool? You buy
a crappy, scratchy,
certainly Suffolk
sweater because you like
the pretty color,
then brag that you're too sensitive
to wear wool.
What do you know
of merino, Spanish wool so fine
it makes a grandmother's love
seem cold and harsh?
Men were beheaded
for smuggling these sheep.
You could spend a life
exploring the differences
between Icelandic and Churro,
Black Welsh Mountain,
Finn, Romney, Jacob, Corriedale,
Karakul, Cheviot, Shetland, Lincoln, Leicester—
both Border and Blue-Faced—

Coopworth, Cormo, Targhee, Wensleydale,
Herdwick, Swaledale,
Cotswold, God forbid,
Dorset, Tunis, Polworth, Rambouillet.
Then begin on rare breeds.
Don't get me started.

Wool is the perfect fiber,
the only one
which insulates when wet.
Wet cotton, silk,
are out to save themselves, leaching
your body heat away.
Like us, wool breathes.
Unlike us, it's blessed with memory,
returns to its original shape when washed.
Wool is proof of a benign, personal God;
is grace, divine intervention at its best.
It's why sheep are mentioned in the Bible
more than any other animal.
I made that up,
but you believed me, proving
you've had your own suspicions
all along.

When mercury freezes,
hang your quilts on the wall.
Curl under wool.
Wool knows you're a mammal.
It's sympathetic, doesn't just conserve
body heat—it radiates it,

melting your bunched muscles
into something capable of sleep,
making sure your dreams
fill with green fields.

Why I Spin
Deborah Robson

I don't have time to spin, but I told two friends I would join them for an afternoon with our wheels. The mortgage is due, and the manuscript I'm supposed to be editing sits on the table like a block of granite. I said I'd meet an emergency deadline. I said I'd spin. I'll do both. I said I would.

So I shove the chair closer to the table and reach past it for one of my two wheels, the one that has already survived many thousands of miles and yards of yarn. This is the wheel I learned on, the wheel I've taught with, the wheel I don't worry about. It's the old one. Ashford wheels, like cars, evolve over the years. Mine (the Traditional) is the simplest model, the earliest.

When I got it, years ago, the only way anyone knew to acquire a spinning wheel was to order a dozen from New Zealand, so a group of us did. All of us wove; some knitted; none was a spinner. We were all curious.

My box looked like everyone else's. I opened one long end and lifted the opposite side, and the nested pieces gently slid out: the wheel, the legs, the treadle, and the flat boards that would hold everything together. The tapered maidens, the spherical knobs, the square-edged treadle supports.

The instructions suggested finishing the parts before assembly. I chose a slow process: fruitwood stain, and then French polish. I rubbed in four coats of dilute shellac and linseed oil, smoothed the wood's surface between coats, and finally burnished it with paste wax. Several in the group used Danish oil. One applied polyurethane. I soon discovered that French polish watermarks and shows wear; it doesn't protect the wood completely. But as time passes, my wheel gathers history. It grows sweeter.

Our group of fledgling spinners took to meeting on Tuesday nights in my living room—an open space with big windows bordered by squares of stained glass, an expanse of wide pine floor boards. Between six and nine of us easily fit there, with chairs and wheels and pungent tea. We spun, we taught ourselves and each other to spin better, and we talked about everything and nothing.

That sense of Tuesday-night community has sustained me since. Although I moved away from that place and those people, both are still part of me. Those experiences affect the way I choose jobs and companions. They have bound themselves into my life the way my cat's short black hairs and my Border collie's silky fur blend invisibly, inevitably, into every yarn I spin now.

The Ashford's treadle cracked during a move, and a friend made a plywood equivalent. I lost the brake knob, and kept spinning by jamming a broken pencil wrapped with masking tape into the hole. Although I bought a real replacement knob eventually, it didn't work right. So I whittled a 4-inch scrap of dowel to a taper and I use that instead. It squeaks a little when I twist it to change the tension, but it serves well, like the mended ligament in my right index finger.

I hoist the wheel out of the corner. I know without thinking where to grasp, how to lift, how to settle the wheel's no-longer-awkward limbs against my own bones, and how to get it through doors without bumping. Tilting the wheel at the correct angle, I lift it into the car.

I love the feel of the fibers I spin, and I'll use and enjoy the yarn. But most of the reasons my old wheel and I drive across town to join the others are invisible.

Incrementalism

Ellen de Graffenreid

My husband believes I am an incrementalist—and he is worried.

While some people might put the cart before the horse, he firmly believes that I have put the dog before the sheep.

About two years ago, I acquired a Pembroke Welsh corgi puppy—a dog with a notoriously strong herding instinct. Cadfael (named after the inquisitive monk created by author Ellis Peters and immortalized by Sir Derek Jacobi in the PBS television series) herds everything. Family members, our Labrador retriever, flocks of birds, and runners on the neighborhood track where we go to exercise—all are fair game. My husband *knows* that sheep are next.

I'm not certain how worried he was at first. My previous

hobby—counted-thread embroidery—was pretty, but he didn't see a lot of practical use for it. He could definitely see the advantages of my learning to knit soon after we relocated to the Pacific Northwest. He believes in my hobbies—after all, I hold down a responsible and challenging job at a major research university, and creative outlets are good for stress. And he could see the side benefit of warm hats, scarves, socks, and mittens.

I think he was even a bit proud as I mastered shaping, cables, and stranded knitting. We live in a rural area, so I often shop on the Internet, but I had a good explanation for each of the packages of yarn and tools as they arrived. Baby sweaters, a request by my stepson for a London beanie, and Christmas knitting all made plausible excuses.

His first hint that something serious was going on was not the accumulation of yarn—even in our small condo, I have my space and he has his. I don't think he was even all that worried by my visits to the booth of a local yarn producer who sells at our farmers' market. Her Icelandic wool is wonderful for this climate, and I let him pick out colors for a hat and mitts that I designed and knit for him.

He wasn't tremendously perturbed by the fact that our local yarn shop owner knows me by name. After all, I took one of my first knitting classes there, and she and her husband are fellow foreign service retirees, so we know people in common from our previous careers.

He even managed to write off my plans to attend an "Alpacapalooza" event with my best girlfriend as a weekend jaunt with one of my eccentric friends who used to own llamas, as well as an excuse to shop in a more urban area.

It may have slowly dawned on him when I insisted on

attending Kate Painter's sheep shearing. Kate owns Paradise Fibers and lives just up the road, so he could have justified my interest as a passing opportunity and due in part to my family's historic commitment to sheep ranching in eastern Montana—after all, he has heard the stories of the time that my cousin accidentally released a shed full of lambs, much to the amusement of the ranch hands.

I think what finally and permanently clued him in was the drop spindle. To the uninitiated, drop spindles don't look like they *do* anything. My attempts to spin on this strange implement were met with amusement. It was a slow process and he didn't think I'd stick it out. But I did.

Then, I brought home a spinning wheel.

We'd received an unexpected financial windfall and agreed that we could each make a major purchase. He bought a computer/printer/fax/scanner. I bought a Lendrum wheel.

Since it was destined to sit in our living room in plain sight, I allowed him some input. He preferred the sleek, Scandinavian lines of the Lendrum maple wheel to the more ornate Kromski minstrel, so I let him think that his opinion influenced the purchase decision. I just didn't have the mental energy to explain the importance of spinning ratios and the merits of double versus single treadle.

I borrowed videos and spent a month or two mastering the wheel. I now produce passable yarn and am spinning up brightly colored samples destined for socks.

My husband tolerates my side trips to fiber stores when I'm traveling on business. A trip to Los Angeles netted three skeins of Koigu painted merino and 1,300 yards of two-ply alpaca yarn. Another time, I came back from Seattle with a plying head for my spinning wheel and a suitcase full of roving.

He even helps me figure out ways to keep the "sheepy-smelling" wool away from the corgi, who is inordinately interested in playing with it. He has accompanied me to a local alpaca ranch's end-of-season sale and good-naturedly puts up with my pointing out fiber-bearing animals from the car windows on weekend trips.

He hasn't said a word about the stacks of scholarly books on prehistoric textiles that I bring home from the university library, or about my excitement in watching a Discovery Channel special about Caucasian mummies in China. The scientists explaining their origins relied heavily on textile evidence—and those were definitely European sheep that produced the wool for the ancient garments.

Academic interest is a superb camouflage for fiber obsession. I justified a fiber-arts retreat by taking classes on Estonian knitting. My husband, a retired foreign service officer, opened the U.S. embassy in Estonia in the mid-1990s and has a strong interest in Baltic cultures. He read Nancy Bush's book, and, even though the retreat occurred on Valentine's Day, he was very understanding about my pilgrimage across the state to take her classes and was thrilled that I met members of our region's Estonian community.

But he is definitely thinking ahead. About two nights ago, out of the blue, he asked, "What about the loom?"

"What loom?" I said innocently.

"I mean it," he said. "What about the loom?"

"Have I said *anything* about a loom?" (Have I mentioned we live in a small condo?)

Maybe I should hide the weaving catalogues behind the other magazines. The corgi won't stay in his basket.

A Rose by Any Other Name

Mari Jane Bartley

"Whoa! It stinks in here," exclaimed Sarah as she entered the house ahead of me. I was close behind when she stopped in her tracks. I'm not sure what hit me first, the smell or the screen door.

"M. J. just got attacked from both ends," roared Marion with her deep rolling laughter. "And for your information, that stink just happens to be the fleece we're supposed to use in the fleece-to-shawl contest." We had gathered at Marion's house to practice for a spinning and weaving competition, which was due to take place in a few days.

A huge heap of brown wool was lying on the rug. "The brown wool will look nice with the ivory-colored warp threads," I said, "but you should have told us that we needed gas masks. I don't recall that it smelled that bad at the farm."

"Well, it's not easy to tell one bad smell from another on a sheep farm on a hot day in July," Marion countered. "I did try hanging it up in the rafters of the barn to air it out, but all that did was frighten the horses. It did keep out the raccoons, though."

Although smell wasn't one of the criteria for judging, this stink was so bad that we knew it would offend the judges. It was against the rules to wash the fleece, so we would need to find another way around the problem.

Sarah, who raises sheep, offered, "I have lots of wool if you don't mind using white."

"Can't do that," Marion grumbled. "If we use white we'll lose our pattern."

"We can't use any of my fleeces; they've all been washed," I replied. Then the idea hit me, like the screen door and the smell. "Hey, there's no rule against using a fleece that we've used before. Joan may still have the black lamb fleece that we used last fall."

And so, early one warm Saturday in August, I placed a basket of shiny black lamb fleece into my van next to my spinning wheel, and set off to pick up the other spinners.

Charlotte had been definite in giving me directions to her place. "You'll see two tire tracks going up an embankment into the woods. Just wait there. The path is too treacherous to drive up to the house." I parked the car on the road, and soon the seventy-year-old appeared, pushing a wheelbarrow piled high. I put her things in my van while Charlotte tucked the wheelbarrow behind a tree.

On to Sarah's place. She emerged from the house wearing jeans, a red gingham shirt, and a red bandanna—our costume for the contest. Her husband, Will, loaded her spinning wheel into my van. "You'd better drive carefully," he said, grinning. "If the police stop you, they'll think you're on your way to a *Hee Haw* reunion."

An hour later, we were unloading our equipment at the fairgrounds. Looking toward the faraway barn where the competition was to be held, Charlotte said, "We should've brought the wheelbarrow with us." We nodded in agreement as we lugged our stuff through the rising heat of late morning.

"At least we aren't hauling that smelly fleece," I commented. Sarah and I proceeded to recount the story of the foul-smelling wool to Charlotte, who has raised sheep for most of her life.

"It must have been from an old ram," Charlotte informed us. "The older they get, the stronger they smell." Mystery solved.

Inside, the huge red barn had a carnival atmosphere. We walked past pens of frisky lambs and kid goats, wire cages stuffed with fluffy rabbits, and vendors selling wool, yarn, and spinning wheels.

"There's Marion," Sarah exclaimed, pointing to a woman setting up her loom.

Marion greeted us. "It's about time you showed up. We've got fifteen minutes to get ready. I brought a fan so we won't die in this heat. Just be careful where it's aimed; we don't want our fleece to blow away."

Three teams were competing in the contest. Each consisted of three spinners and a weaver, but we also had Bill, Marion's husband, who acted as our coach. He was indispensable and very much appreciated for his ability to lower the anxiety level with his dry wit and off-the-wall jokes.

The judges reviewed the rules before we began. We had three hours to spin yarn and weave a 20-by-72-inch shawl. The shawls were to be judged on the consistency of the spun yarn, the consistency of the weaving, the quality of the fleece, and the difficulty of the pattern. Marks were also awarded for the teams' appearance and displays.

The starting bell rang, and we were off. Using wire-bristled combing cards, we teased the ebony wool into soft, lofty pillows. After amassing a dozen pillows of fluff, the spinners began treadling their wheels, twisting a shiny soft yarn onto the bobbin with a flick of the wrist. As the bobbins filled, we transferred the yarn to the weaving shuttle. Marion began to treadle the loom, lifting each of the harnesses in turn to create the chosen pattern. All around us rose the quiet whirring of the wheels, the steady beat of the looms, the far-off baas and buzz of clippers shearing sheep.

The first hour raced past as we worked frantically.

"Slow down! I don't want anyone passing out from heat exhaustion," urged Bill as he handed us cups of water. "We're halfway there, so take your time."

Once our pace slowed, we could chat with spectators and each other. We took turns whining at Marion, "How much longer?"

Finally she said, "You can stop spinning and whining now, but get ready to tie the fringe." We cut the shawl from the loom and used overhand knots to secure the loose ends. After dunking the shawl in a bucket of sudsy water, we rinsed, towel-dried, and ironed it. We all watched, breath held, as Marion measured. Was it the regulation size? It was.

It was also a work of art. The black yarn provided the perfect background for the ivory rosebuds created by the pattern—far better than brown would have been. The judges must have agreed with us, because our shawl won first place.

"Not only does it look good, but it smells good, too," Sarah proclaimed.

Charlotte added, "I guess it was a good thing that the brown fleece stank so badly, because the black fleece ended up smelling like a rose."

Just in case you're wondering whatever happened to the stinky fleece: Marion abandoned it on my doorstep. After a good wash, it made a fine, cozy felt jacket.

Stuffing
Rena Trefman Cobrinik

My beautiful souvenirs stood in my living room like four large floppy hatboxes. The four leather hassocks that I'd brought back from a week in Morocco had been nested into one another for packing. Now unfolded, they wobbled, empty except for memories, waiting to be stuffed.

Zambia, a guide and family friend, had been invaluable in helping me find just the right hassocks for my children's family: one for myself, one in a perfect shade of green for my children, and two smaller hassocks for my granddaughters. The smaller ones had patterns as complex as Persian rugs, woven with strips of bright blue, green, orange, and white leather, Tangier-style.

Looking at them, I found myself back in the open-air Moroccan market, near booths shielded from the hot sun by makeshift canvas or aluminum awnings. The robed women sat silent and busy, with children sleeping in shawls on their backs. Men were responding to an unspoken call to prayer, using pitchers or bowls for ritual washing. Around me, a bewildering array of colors shouted in their intensity. In cartons, on shelves, piled high were mounds of exotic foods—

dried fruits, warm pita bread, nuts and herbs, fresh fruits and vegetables. But it all stayed picturelike; the dry air carried few smells in the cave-like area, its stalls divided by narrow dirt passages. The muted conversations I could not catch, the wares inside and outside, the toppling piles of pots and pans, the fine leather goods—all seemed to be behind an invisible yet impenetrable barrier. Only when I saw Zambia, smiling at me as he embraced a merchant or accepted a sample date or fig, did I feel that this place was real.

Suddenly, a friend of Zambia's threaded his way through the maze of stalls, carrying a hassock. I'd almost given up hope of finding one to go with a newly upholstered chair at home. The hassock had a pattern of black flowers embroidered on wine-red leather. It was so lovely that I felt a guilty pleasure. Mine was the most beautiful hassock of all.

When I thanked Zambia for his patience and kindness, and for the pleasure he seemed to take in being my guide, he gave me his generous smile and said in his halting English, "The best stuffing is sheep's wool. Be sure the wool is dry."

Now, back in the United States, I remembered his instructions. Sheep's wool should be easy. A friend of mine, who lived only a few miles away, raised sheep. He had bags and bags of wool.

"Anytime—as much as you want," my friend assured me. I could tell he was relieved to get rid of a bagful. "Just soak it overnight in the bathtub and dry it near the stove."

"Sure," I answered doubtfully. Once home, it took all my strength to lift the bag out of my car's trunk. It must have weighed at least 20 pounds. I had no idea how I was going to get the wool from the black garbage bag into my beautiful hassocks. But when I opened the bag and looked at the wool, I knew one thing: This was not going in my bathtub. Sheep don't live indoors, and the wool made it clear why they shouldn't.

It was December 1, and I wanted to get the hassocks ready as holiday gifts. Time for action. I phoned Fosterfields, a model nineteenth-century farm in Morristown, New Jersey, where I'd seen a sheep-shearing exhibit. The woman in charge, trying to be helpful, made me realize how little I knew. What kind of wool was it? From what breed of sheep? I had no idea; I only knew they'd been delicious at the Rotary picnic. How many pounds of wool did I need to wash? Subsequent discussion made it clear that I had too little of the stuff to take it for professional washing. She gave me the name and number of a spinners' organization that might know more, and added, "I think you soak it in the bathtub overnight."

By the time I called the spinner, I had done my homework. I knew the wool was from Dorset, Suffolk, and Hampshire sheep. The spinner sighed. "Those are meat sheep, not wool sheep. The wool's not worth sending for professional washing." She gave me the washer's phone number anyway. "If you're in a rush, just soak it in the bathtub overnight."

After making my way through a maze of voice-mail options, I learned that the wool-washing company was at least a four-hour trip away and wouldn't be open till spring.

Here, on the cusp of the twenty-first century, there had to be a more high-tech solution than the bathtub. I turned to the Internet for more ideas.

Soon, I'd downloaded and printed out almost fifty pages. I never knew that wool washing was such a complex operation. It wasn't just that it was a lot of work; it seemed I'd need a lot of stuff. My first printout listed orders for soaps, including one that would make the wool smell like jasmine (something to think about). And there it was, on the soap-order page: "Soak the wool in the bathtub overnight."

What are laundromats for, anyway? I found one a few towns away and used the largest machine for a trial run with a small portion of the wool.

As I watched the wool and soapy water slosh round and round behind the glass window, I struggled with guilt. If I were an honest person, my wool would be soaking in the bathtub. What would the laundromat people say or (worse) do to me if they found out? The suds emptied, the machine spun and then slowed to a stop. Oh, bliss! The dirty gray wool was a beautiful creamy yellow.

"It washed right out!" I almost shouted. What a relief. They wouldn't throw me out. I had a solution. Simple soap and water made me feel like an honest person. I flung open the washing machine door and reached in.

The scrungy, soft tufts of wool had matted into hardened strips of felt. And there was so little of it! I'd spent more than six dollars on a fraction of the wool I'd need. It wasn't even completely clean; some of the mud (I'd decided it was mud) hadn't come out.

At home, I carefully reread the pages I'd downloaded from the Internet. The pages agreed on the essentials. The soap part was important: Dawn and Arm & Hammer washing soda (not easy to find in my neighborhood) were the brands of choice. Bathtub soaking was a given. The water should be hot at first. After a couple of rinses in the tub, it would be okay to use the washing machine on a slow spin to get rid of excess water without felting the wool.

Reconciled to the inevitable, I left the wool to soak in the bathtub for a few hours. At first, it seemed to rest on top of the water like a cloud that had settled down on a pond. It refused to be rushed. Kneeling on the bathroom floor, leaning over the edge of the tub, and working out the debris of mud and weeds, I thought of the quiet women in the Tangier market and the narrow passages between the stalls. Alone in my high-tech world, I found comfort with them. My American bathroom had acquired a productiveness of its own. It was, I suppose, a market stall of sorts.

The water slowly turned brown. There; I *knew* it was mud. I rinsed the wool and watched the soil granules drift down the drain. More soap. Another rinse. The wool grew paler and paler. I lifted it, played with it, so soft, so creamy white. The mud acted as a natural abrasive; it and the soap left the tub gleaming white.

It took me a day to find the mesh bags I needed to hold the wool for machine spinning. Two bags fit nicely into the machine, and the gentle cycle spun most of the water out. As instructed, I'd made drying stations by setting up screens on well-spaced cardboard cartons. I thought again of market stalls. Over the next few days, bits of grass and twigs filtered down. Dander flew; the house smelled of drying mittens and sweaters moist with spring rain.

I had to wash the wool a little at a time. Eventually I would snip out the really solid bits of mud which I learned wouldn't wash out. Each time, I'd sink my hands with pleasure into the floating wool. I remembered the disappointment of touching cotton candy; it looked like clouds, but it felt sticky if you touched it with anything but your tongue. Wet wool was softer than anything I'd ever touched.

I wrapped three empty hassocks in gift paper. As my family tore the packages open, I brought out my three white plastic bags of home-washed wool, singing the obvious nursery rhyme. There still wasn't enough to fill all three hassocks. They're still waiting.

A friend told me that she'd filled the hassocks she'd bought in Turkey, ten years ago, with crumpled newspapers. "It works very well," she said. "They're still firm."

No; that wouldn't do for my hassocks. Not good enough. It may be a while before I'm ready for the pleasures of washing wool again, and so it may be a while before we can use my beautiful souvenirs. But in my mind's ear, I still hear Zambia, in the crowded market, leaning toward me and saying, "Sheep's wool is best."

In the Old Days
Marcy Moffet

Not many people know that in the old days, they didn't dye wool to make it different colors the same way we do now. Nowadays, we dye the wool before it's spun into yarn, or we dye the yarn before it has been woven or knit into fabric, or we dye the fabric before it has been made into a garment. All of which can be messy, time-consuming, and even hazardous. But in the old days, in the country places, they didn't do it the way we do now. They had a better way.

I'm privileged to know two experienced shepherds named

Jim and Harry who have a big old sheep farm in the Catskill Mountains of New York State. They have several hundred sheep that they keep for the wool, the meat, and the milk.

Now, Jim and Harry still practice many of the old ways, and they have shared some of their secrets with me. Not *all* their secrets with me; they've been very cagey. They guard the old ways well. They haven't told me enough so that I could go out and do it myself; but they've told me enough to give me an idea of how it was done.

Jim and Harry say that in the old days they used to dye the sheep's wool while it was still on the sheep—on the *living* sheep. First they'd decide what colors they wanted to produce that year—say, navy, red, and green. Then, right after the spring shearing, they would separate the sheep to be tinted into groups and keep them in separate paddocks until the next shearing.

Every day the shepherd would add a dose of tincture to the water of the sheep, a different tincture for each tinting group, and the sheep would have no water without the tincture. The recipes for tinctures they used are a deep, dark secret; I couldn't get either Jim or Harry to budge on this part. But I think the tinctures were made with herbs, roots, barks, and flowers found around about the farm, in much the same way that folks used to, and sometimes still do, produce natural dyestuffs.

From shearing to shearing, the sheep in the tinting groups would drink the water with the tincture, and as the fleece grew out, it would grow out in red or in blue or in green, depending on the tincture the shepherd had put in the sheep's drinking water. And at the end of the year when the fleece was shorn, it would already be the desired color.

And that's how they did it in the old days.
Or so Jim and Harry tell me.

Color Hunger
Betty Christiansen

The winter I moved from New York to Minnesota, I armed myself for a cold and colorless stretch with loads of colored wool. Having grown up in the Midwest, I knew what to expect: long days of dormancy, with tired, empty light. The predominant color outside would be white or (more often in recent years) gray-brown.

In a box marked OPEN FIRST, I packed skeins of orange-flecked gold wool, a rainbow of kettle-dyed autumn-hued hanks, and a famous stash of homegrown wool dyed red, which I'd bought at the New York Sheep and Wool Festival that fall. I'd gotten it from a woman who'd dyed it to match tomatoes she'd picked the summer before, tomatoes that ultimately were shipped to New Orleans to be cooked up in Emeril Lagasse's kitchen. She had countless shades of red wool for sale, most of them not-quite-successful attempts to capture that exact tomato shade. The particular lot I was drawn to was the batch that hit the mark. When I heard that tomato story, I couldn't let the wool go. I bought all she had in that shade.

As I packed my wool, I packed with it my intentions for coping with a long, dark, and drab winter, prime time for a hibernatory habit like knitting. This tomato wool, with the other brilliant shades carefully tucked into boxes with lavender and cedar sachets, would defend me against the doldrums. I would have summer, warmth, and color at my fingertips.

This wasn't the first time I'd relied upon color to see me through a dark and dreary spell. Years ago, when I left an alcoholic fiancé, the balm to my spirit was an airy mohair pullover, dyed in eye-popping 1980s fuchsia, purple, and turquoise. The fluffy fiber felt indulgent, a cushion in a particularly rocky time. The color was itself a celebration. Knitting with it reminded me that, despite the confusion and depression I was enduring, the future held promise.

Maybe five years after that—years including happy single ones—I found myself pulled toward a gorgeous sea-blue wool. I knew that an Aran sweater in that wool would look spectacular with my new sweetheart's blond hair and deep hazel eyes. I knit the sweater for him, and as we fingered its cables and bobbles we dreamed of the ocean, of traveling, of sharing a life that was far from ordinary. He still has it, and has worn it on some of the adventures that we continue to have.

I've always loved knitting and wool and colors, bright or subdued; but only recently, colors have begun to move me in a different way. Some people say that colors have healing properties, that certain shades stimulate certain centers of the brain or make you vibrate at a particular frequency. I wouldn't know about that, but there's no doubt that certain colors, or combinations of colors, make me (and perhaps other people) feel good.

I began to notice, for example, that if I walked into a quilt shop, I couldn't leave without investing in a good-sized stack of fat quarters. I wasn't driven by the need to pad a fabric stash; in fact, I've never stitched a quilt. It was just that I couldn't resist the appeal of pulling these neat little parcels off shelves, setting French blues against maizes, gathering fistfuls of pumpkins and junipers and bricks and gold, gorging on candy pinks and limes and bright, fizzy yellows. I'd bring my treasures to the cash register and lay them out on the counter in neat little rainbows. Sometimes the shopkeeper would comment on my choices, sometimes not. No matter—the thrill was in their particular appeal to me, however momentary, and in my possession of them.

This might explain the recent exponential growth of my yarn stash, too. More and more often, I find myself giving in to that ball of hand-painted sock yarn in orange and green and gold, those hanks of midnight blue and cranberry red and brushed bronze, those skeins of daylily and rhubarb, those balls of creamy white and warm brown-gray with names like Moonshadow that make me swoon. I dream of the longed-for day when I finally have time to knit them up. Until then, I squirrel them away, taking them out from time to time to stare at them, combinations so pleasing I can't avert my eyes.

This accumulation has not been without guilt. I confessed as much one day to Claudia, the owner of a yarn store I used to frequent in upstate New York. "It's not like I need more yarn," I told her as I walked in, drawn like a moth to flame (or to wool). "But I just love the colors. I can't get enough. I want to rip it all down and take a *bath* in it." I couldn't make eye contact as I spoke to her, too dazzled by the kaleidoscope on her shelves. "I don't even want to knit with it. I just want to possess it. Isn't that terrible?"

"Not at all," she shot back, absolving me. "Sometimes that's the whole point. What's wrong with collecting yarn just to inspire, to make you feel good, to give you something to think about and plan with? Whether you actually knit with it is irrelevant." She went on to describe the baskets of wool in her own home, carefully and artfully arranged to reflect the season or her mood, or simply because the yarns made surprising combinations. Their colors stimulate the hunger to create, fill the mind to bursting with possibility, and offer a sense of promise, of hope.

I didn't forget Claudia's wise words. When my husband (he of the sea-blue sweater) and I entered our new space in southeastern Minnesota—the Mississippi River bordering our backyard, bald eagles plunging and soaring from its bluffs—I found and opened that box of tomato-colored wool. I bundled it into a basket with the deep gray Moonshadow and a thick, creamy blend of mohair, silk, and wool. It was a crisp, pleasing arrangement that nevertheless made me homesick for the region I'd just left and the farms, festivals, and spinneries these skeins had come from.

The basket of wool served as a sort of sad memento until one morning when, knitting in the wan light from a window overlooking our new backyard, I looked out and saw the bare branches of certain bushes sagging with bright berries—the same red as my tomato yarn—against dark bark and white snow. Without realizing it, I'd collected the colors of my new home and put them together in one basket: a celebration of the future and the inherent possibilities.

Winter is over now, and the berries are gone, ravished in a single day by a flock of hungry cedar waxwings. Driven by hunger of a different kind, I find myself ransacking my stash in hopes of capturing the present: the fresh green haze veiling the trees, the blue river, the pale gold pooling in marshland reeds, the yellow flame of forsythia and the blaze of tulips; the air, the wind, the sky, the sun—all in a basket of wool.

Cauldrons of Color
Janette Ryan-Busch

Summer is almost gone, and my house is starting to look like a witch's cottage. Coming home, I'm greeted by bucket after bucket of walnuts oozing brown juices into sun-warmed water. The old weathered porch is hung with drying plants. Along each of the porch's band joists hang freshly dyed skeins of yarn. A massive kettle of wool and alum sits cooling just outside the door. Step inside, and you'll inhale a curious mix of smells: the distinct bite of indigo, working its blue spell, mingles with the spicy tang of marigold.

My hundred-year old faded gray farmhouse didn't used to look like this. But in fall, curious things happen when a person has a house full of fiber and a flock in the field. For decades, I'd noticed how berry picking left my hands stained with purple, how the green husks of walnuts turned the driveway brown each year. Now that fleeces and skeins were filling my house and life, I made trips to the library. I read a winter's worth of books and went to a three-day symposium on natural dyes. A whole new world opened up before me as familiar plants on the farm took on a new significance.

That first spring, growing my dye garden was a revelation. March came, and I stumped my gardening friends with mystery plants sprouting under grow lights and trailing along the window sills. In June, the young woad plants looked so much like dandelions that I had to post DO NOT WEED signs to save them from well-intentioned gardening friends.

I learned, that year, to play with a spectrum of yellows, from the soft subtleties of carrot tops to the electric hues of marigold blooms. I filled in the chromatic gaps with chamomile, asters, and goldenrod in all its stages, from early spring shoots to fall flowers. My big canning pot spent the whole summer simmering away, as I searched out the largest strainers I could find in town. Our well water is hard enough to pave with, so I lugged home bottled water.

In June, my grandmother's dark red hollyhocks—hauled from farm to farm in my transient days—began to bloom. I picked fresh flowers every afternoon from the 7-foot stalks, until my drying racks overflowed and spilled burgundy petals onto the floor. Later that month, as a full moon rose, I brewed a fine concoction of hollyhock, alum, and distilled water. By midnight I had purple skeins, purple spoons, and one purple dishtowel.

I robbed the blackbirds of mulberries that summer. Perched on a ladder poked through the mulberry tree's snarled branches, I stripped out fruit as the birds shrilly objected overhead. After three days' mulberry-fermentation, I dyed my wool a cotton-candy pink. I hung it from the tree to dry, but the birds were not impressed.

On the eve of the summer solstice, I soaked sunflower heads overnight and harvested nettles. At dawn the next day, I added a good pinch of copper to each pot and caught the greens of summer. The soft sage yarn dyed with the nettle brew hung next to the deeper, duskier green of skeins infused in sunflower juice.

By August, I had mastered the alchemy of indigo and woad. Woad came out cornflower blue if I packed gallon jars extra tight with finely chopped leaves before slowly pouring in boiling water, expelling every last air bubble. I built new arm muscles pouring the potion back and forth from pot to pot, to aerate the brew. Yarn left for an hour in indigo came out sparkling sapphire; yarn left overnight emerged the color of stormy skies. I had yarn in shades from robin's egg to cobalt and everything in between.

In January's pallid days, I pulled out madder root, shipped from my friend Bab's garden in California. I fermented the twisted crimson roots in a limy brew, as winter whitewashed the landscape as far as I could see. A week later, I conjured fine reds and oranges strong enough to rival a summer sunset and hung my skeins, shouting color to a gray-white world.

Today, I have picked blossoms and leaves from the marigold hedge at the back edge of my dye garden. I have simmered them in kettles that filled the house with spicy scent and strained off the golden broth, pouring it back and forth. A good pinch of copper turned the brew a beautiful emerald green. My skeins are soaking now, as I write.

Soon, the first frosts will put an end to summer gardens, but I know the cold nights will make elderberries and pokeweed ready to charm wool into magenta. My neighbors will, of course, shake their heads, roll their eyes, and continue to question my sanity as they pass me pulling plants in the ditch of this meandering road. I will pack bag after bag into the freezer, knowing that they'll be there as a steady comfort through the winter, when I get to work on the half-dozen summer fleeces, washed and bagged and waiting on the loom-room shelf.

Winter may bleach the world, but I have my ways of decanting summer, all winter long.

About the Editors and Contributors

Rosanne Anderson shares a small ranch with her husband, a few cows, sheep, retired carriage horses, and lots of cats and dogs. She loves all aspects of fiber art, especially preparing raw wool for projects. In her spare time she teaches middle school and does freelance writing.

Sheila Anderson lives in the north of England. She has worked at the local university but now pursues her other interests—writing, family history, reading, theater, and socializing. She has recently won two writing competitions held by a local Authors' Circle. She is married with four children and one grandson.

Susan Atkinson lives in Norman, Oklahoma, with her husband, son, and daughter. She has been knitting fearlessly for twenty years. After intending to be a writer since high school, she was published for the first time in 2002.

Jeannine Bakriges keeps a tea bag "fortune" that reads, "'You will do foolish things, but do them with enthusiasm.'—Colette." This suits her. A passionate fiber artist and teacher, she also co-owns (with Susan Krahling) The Copper Moth, selling naturally dyed fibers to handspinners (http://www.coppermoth.com).

After learning to knit and crochet in the same day, Ohioan **Mari Jane Bartley** continues to try all types of fiber techniques. She has enjoyed working with Convergence 2000 and the Fiberfest Festival. However, her fondest fiber memories are of spinning in fleece-to-shawl competitions.

Christine Basham is a freelance writer and homeschooling mother of four. She lives in Maryland, where you can get by without a sweater most of the year. After a decade of needle-phobia, she recently took up knitting again. It's easier with margaritas.

Zoë Blacksin does most of her knitting at Yale University, where she wrote "A Glossary of Knitting" as an escape from exams. This fall she returns to school as an art history major. Zoë is a native of Greenfield, Massachusetts, where she knits, reads, and writes with her family.

Janet Blowney has been knitting since childhood and has the stash to prove it. She participates in local and global efforts to "knit the world warm." She works as a technical editor to support her yarn habit.

Jef Buehler has knit exactly three rows for what may never become a felted purse for his wife. He knits words—usually poetry—for a wide variety of media. He works in the field of downtown revitalization and practices and teaches Kundalini yoga in and around Trenton, New Jersey.

Carole Ann Camp, an ordained minister with a doctorate in science education, has written books on women in science, edited books on women's sermons, and coauthored a book on labyrinths. She paints, sings, plays piano, tap-dances, quilts, knits, crochets, embroiders, needlepoints, and sews everything from banners to wedding dresses.

Betty Christiansen is a freelance writer and editor who lives with her husband, Andrew, in southeastern Minnesota. A frequent contributor to *Interweave Knits*, *Vogue Knitting*, and *Family Circle Easy Knitting*, Betty has been knitting since the age of eight, and has recently received an M.F.A. in nonfiction writing from Sarah Lawrence College.

Charmian Christie lives and writes in Guelph, Ontario, where she shares a century home with her husband and half a dozen unfinished knitting projects. Her stories appear in print and online, and have been heard on CBC national radio. Charmian recently abandoned amateur acting to be humbled as a playwright.

Lorraine Lener Ciancio is a poet, writer, photographer, and knitter. Her work has appeared in anthologies and publications and also (a sweater design!) in *Interweave Knits*. She lives in Taos, New Mexico, with her artist husband and dog Spike, and is at work on a memoir and a collection of poems.

A New England native, **Laurie Clark** has filled her life and her heart with everything from cats and dogs to angora rabbits and sheep. She dreams of owning alpacas as she spins, weaves, knits, sews, paints, reupholsters, and creates porcelain dolls. In her spare time she teaches high school English.

Nancy Clark may not be a fabulously talented knitter, but she sheepishly admits she can spin a good yarn, especially when it comes to needling her wool-gathering students.

E. B. Clutter lives in Toronto. Although her own knitting never progressed past the scarf stage, she's always been close to wonderful knitters—her mother, the friend of her story, and her daughter, who knits jewelry from fine wire of silver and gold.

Rena Trefman Cobrinik taught in New York and New Jersey. Her writing has appeared in the *New York Times*, *Jersey Woman*, *Packentragen*, and *The Jewish Women's Literary Annual*. She and her husband live in the woods of northern New Jersey, where she shovels snow, gardens, and makes soups.

Suzanne Cody knits and writes amid the chaos of her Iowa City home.

Claudia Conner was taught to knit when she was thirty by a twelve-year old girl. Her current hobby is knitting and giving away baby sweaters—more than fifty so far. Claudia recently graduated summa cum laude from Fordham University with a bachelor of arts at the age of fifty-eight.

Ellen de Graffenreid lives with her family, her Pembroke Welsh corgi, and a benevolent Labrador retriever in Pullman, Washington. She supports her fiber obsession by communicating on behalf of Washington State University and is aided and abetted by the community of part-time and full-time fiber artists living on the Palouse.

Laurie Doran, who designed her first sweaters in her teens with her mother's guidance, lives in Maine with her husband. She does freelance writing, sells her sweaters at craft sales and art galleries, and teaches knitting classes. She aims to become a master climber and gives slide shows on mountaineering.

Marie Dorian is a writer and recent knitter who lives in Lynchburg, Virginia. In 2000, she joined the Virginia Organizing Project. It is a statewide grassroots organization dedicated to challenging injustice by empowering people in local communities. After facilitating removal of racist bas-reliefs from a courthouse, contributing to *KnitLit* was easy.

Kay Dorn, a retired writer, lives on Cape Cod with her husband. They enjoy canoeing, kayaking, biking, and walking. She is a volunteer for the Brewster Ladies' Library—mostly writing, editing, transcribing, and proofreading whenever the need arises.

Kathryn Eike Dudding, who lives in Clifton Park, New York, tells stories throughout the northeastern states. Whether sharing participation stories with three-year-olds, creating stories set in history for all ages, or singing old-time songs with senior citizens, she delights in the joy and understanding she sees in the faces of her audiences.

Kelly Elayne was born and raised in Connecticut and is currently immersed in the Los Angeles world of music video and commercial production. Her fiction has appeared in *Tarpaulin Sky*, *Lean Seed*, *House Taken Over*, *Storyglossia*, *Poetry Midwest*, and *Coloring Book*, an anthology from Rattlecat Press.

Although **Jay Elliott**'s hands are hopeless with knitting needles, he shines in flashing hand signals as a summer baseball umpire in western Massachusetts. During the school year he wears handknit sweaters (now with sleeves) to work as a member of the English department at Clark University in Worcester, Massachusetts.

Jenny Feldon works full-time to support her yarn and yoga addictions. She spends many hours dropping stitches with her patient teachers at Putting on the Knitz in Newton, Massachusetts. A recent graduate of Boston University, Jenny lives in Boston with her longtime boyfriend and a cat who hates knitting.

Jenny Frost learned to knit from her grandmother when she was seven and has been at it with varying degrees of intensity (and a steadily growing stash) ever since. She has a very tolerant husband and the three best children in the world. She works in publishing in Manhattan.

Dawn Goldsmith learned to knit as a Girl Scout. Between stitches, she writes features for a variety of magazines, including *The Christian Science Monitor* and *Skirt!* magazine. Her work has been published in a number of anthologies.

Kathryn Gunn is an Australian who has never owned a car. She uses her journeys on public transport to indulge in her passion for knitting and encourage others to knit. She is currently writing a book of patterns for vests, most of which have been knitted on trains.

Natalie Harwood raised five children and taught Latin and English at the high school and college levels. She has published short stories, articles on teaching Latin, and *The Complete Idiot's Guide to Learning Latin,* now in its second edition. She is working on a simplified Latin text of Aesop's Fables and knitting snowflakes.

Nancy Huebotter is a technical writer/editor for the defense industry and an aspiring novelist, drawing on story lines from her second avocation—genealogy. Seldom without a project on her needles, she has created sweaters and afghans, endeavoring to keep friends and family warm from birth to maturity.

Abha Iyengar studied economics, practiced interior design, and now pursues writing with a passion. She has been published in print as well as online. She lives with her family in New Delhi, India. She loves knitting everything—sweaters, tales, or relationships. Other interests are yoga, spirituality, reading, and travel.

Donna Jaffe has been knitting for forty years, ever since she learned from her grandmother at age eighteen. She remembers a time she and her little daughter were getting ready to visit friends, and her daughter remarked with a little sigh, "My mama with her knitting."

Perri Klass, a Boston pediatrician, writes for *Knitter's Magazine* and *Parenting*. She has won five O. Henry awards for short fiction. Her most recent books include *Quirky Kids: Understanding and Helping Your Child Who Doesn't Fit In* (with Eileen Costello) and *The Mystery of Breathing*, a novel. Visit http://www.reachoutand-read.org/about_who.html.

Jody Kolodzey is a journalist, photographer, and ethnomusicologist living in Philadelphia. She learned to knit from her mother and developed her skills while attending graduate school in Ireland, where she spent nearly as much time knitting and talking with traditional knitters as she did in the library.

Miriam Lang Budin's first knitting project was a ghastly pair of baby blue slippers produced at the age of nine. She is an accomplished embroiderer and created a freehand crewel representation of her childhood home. She is a librarian in Chappaqua and lives with her husband and sons in Hastings-on-Hudson, New York.

Christine Lavin is a singer/songwriter/guitarist/concert performer/ recording artist/knitter who performs all over the world. She took her first knitting class on October 1, 2002, was instantly hooked, and now includes preshow knitting circles before all her concerts. Visit her at www.christinelavin.com.

Michael Learmond lives in North Wales (UK) with his wife, Gill, and his two children. He started writing because he thought it looked easy and continued to write when he found it wasn't. He has never attempted to knit, however, because that really does look complicated!

Janis Leona lives in Bemidji, Minnesota, with her daughter, Chloe, and two cairn terriers. She teaches writing on the Leech Lake Ojibwe Reservation in northern Minnesota. She has published in various literary magazines, and her plays are performed by local theater groups. "I think, therefore I knit," she says.

Dayna Macy is a writer living in Berkeley, California. Her essays have appeared in *Self, Yoga Journal*, and *Tricycle*, and on Salon.com, where this piece originally appeared.

Tara Jon Manning has an M.A. in textile and apparel design with a specialty in fiber arts. She is a knitwear designer and author, contributing designs to knitting magazines and yarn companies. She owns Tara Handknitting Designs (www.tarahandknitting.com). She and her family live in Boulder, Colorado.

Adrienne Martini has been a theater technician, apprentice massage therapist, bookstore bookkeeper, and pizza joint waitress. She has written for *Cooking Light* and *Interweave Knits*. During the day, she is gainfully employed teaching in Onconta, New York. At all hours, she is mom to Maddy and wife to Scott.

Chris Mastin can't match her mother's fanaticism for knitting and knitwear design but does enjoy knitting scarves as a distraction from her M.F.A.-in-creative-writing homework and her job as a technical writer. She lives in Missoula, Montana, with her Alabama-born husband, their dog, and two cats.

Jamie McNeely writes and knits in northern New Jersey, where she works in a public library as well as her local yarn shop. Although she didn't knit her first stitch until she was almost twenty-four, she did manage to earn degrees in writing from Rowan University and Sarah Lawrence College.

Stephen Mead is a published writer and artist living in northeastern New York. A résumé and samples of his work can be seen at www.123soho.com/members/stephen_mead, www.absolutearts.com /portfolios/s/stephenmead, and www.scars.tv/ccdissues/mead htm

Cuban-born **Nilda Mesa** worked in government and politics as an environmental and international lawyer and policy wonk for almost twenty years. She now does abstract painting and sculpture in Manhattan and France. For examples of her work, see www.toastartwalk.com/nildamesa.html.

Marcy Moffet was born in Colorado many years ago, now lives in western Massachusetts, and is owned by a Maremma sheepdog named Oley. She started knitting in 1988 and spinning in 1985 and hasn't been the same since. She spends her free time consorting with other spinners and knitters and with shepherds and their sheep.

Kathy Myers works in a delinquency prevention program. She lives with her partner of seventeen years, Lisa, and their two beloved yellow Labs, Kiely and Emma. She never leaves the house without knitting needles in her briefcase and also enjoys spinning at her wheel and with her drop spindles.

Lesléa Newman lives in Northampton, Massachusetts. She has written forty books for adults and children, including *Hachiko Waits*; *Cats, Cats, Cats!*; and *The Best Short Stories of Lesléa Newman*. The one vest she knitted shrank in the wash and became a cat bed. Visit www.lesleanewman.com and http://www.leasleakids.com to learn more.

Donna Nothe-Choiniere lives in Princeton, Massachusetts, with thirteen Romney sheep, seven angora rabbits, two rough collies, and one husband. A lifelong knitter and spinner, she likes to experiment with natural dyes, odd fibers, and various cultural styles. Donna teaches spinning, knitting, soapmaking, and plant uses in central Massachusetts.

Christie Nowak shares a cheerful 1920s bungalow in Ann Arbor, Michigan, with her husband, two-year-old son, one dog, and four cats. She divides her time between family, work, and an ever-growing list of hobbies. Her writing has appeared in *Ebbing Tide* and *Sparkles in the Sand*.

Stephanie Pearl-McPhee lives in Toronto with her husband and three daughters, collecting wool, spinning, and avoiding housework. With yarn and needles stashed in every room and at least one project within arm's reach at all times, she aims to elevate knitting to the level of an extreme sport.

Helen Kay Polaski created the Forget Me Knots book series because she loves writing about families. Her first book, *Forget Me Knots from the Front Porch,* is available online and in bookstores. Her work appears in ten anthologies and online. Visit her at www.geocities.com/forgetmeknotsanthology.

Susan Blackwell Ramsey sells books in Kalamazoo, Michigan. Her poetry has been published in *Poetry Northwest, The Indiana Review,* and two anthologies. She teaches spinning and knitting at the Kalamazoo Institute of Arts, where she preaches the Gospel According to Zimmermann.

Deborah Robson took up knitting when she went to college (she vividly remembers the sound of a needle hitting the chapel floor). A former editor of *Spin-Off,* Interweave Press books, and *Shuttle Spindle & Dyepot,* she is now working on a revised edition of Priscilla Gibson-Roberts' classic knitting book.

Stephen D. Rogers grew up watching knitting projects never reach completion but has fared better with his writing, having placed more than 250 of his stories and poems. Visit his website: www.stephendrogers.com.

Linda Roghaar, a native of Massachusetts, has deep ties (yarn and otherwise) to Maine, New Hampshire, and Vermont. She is mother to two grown daughters (both knitters) and owner of the incomparable golden retriever Ellie. She's worked in publishing for many years and is a literary agent in Amherst, Massachusetts.

Sondra Rosenberg has taught college, reviewed restaurants, and coauthored *The Ozarks Traveler* with her husband, Stuart Silverman. Sondra and Stuart now divide their time between Chicago and Hot Springs, Arkansas.

Wren Ross is a singer, actor, designer, and devoted knitter. She's been invited to perform her cabaret, "Singing with Every Fiber!", at the Knit-Out and other wool festivals. (Her CD is called *Wren's Greatest Knits!*) She teaches Story of Fiber, a creative fiber/personal growth workshop. Visit her at www.wrenross.com.

Janette Ryan-Busch lives on a small organic farm outside Iowa City with her husband and a menagerie of fiber animals. She writes, serves on the state organic board, and raises and sells organic flowers and produce. In addition to produce, she sells fiber creations and offers fiber arts courses.

Terry Miller Shannon knits, writes, and gardens on the Oregon coast. She wrote her rhyming children's picture book, *Tub Toys*, with her son, Tim Warner. Her next picture book, *In My Very Own Yard*, will be published in 2005.

Western Massachusetts novelist **Suzanne Strempek Shea**'s first knitting project was a yellow acrylic headband, fashioned at age seven during a 4-H Club meeting. Her latest creation is a memoir, *Songs from a Lead-Lined Room: Notes—High and Low—from My Journey Through Breast Cancer and Radiation* (Beacon Press).

Luke Shiffer, originally from Germany, now lives in Los Angeles, where he strives to fulfill his inextinguishable lust to act. He plans to study law in pursuit of global human rights. Nothing makes him happier than knitting gifts of love for his small, but loving, family.

Micki Smith retired from her career as a public information officer in Maryland to run a Vermont country inn. Retired again, she follows her love of history through old public records researching for a historical novel. She's happiest yarn shopping with her daughter, who inherited the avid knitter gene.

Dana Snyder-Grant is a freelance writer and a social worker, specializing in chronic illness and disability. She is a columnist for her local newspaper in Acton, Massachusetts, where she lives in a cohousing community with her husband and two cats. She no longer knits but she still loves "lit."

Jean Stone is the New England author of ten novels; the latest is *Beach Roses*. Her stories focus on the sometimes reluctant, sometimes mismatched, always rewarding friendships of women romping through life's obstacles and finding strength in each other. Visit www.jeanstone.net.

Martie Stothoff, born in 1993, lives with her parents and sister in western Massachusetts, where she attends elementary school. She joined the school knitting circle at the beginning of third grade. Aside from knitting, she enjoys playing piano and ultimate Frisbee, dancing, and spending time with Ellie the dog.

Janine Tinklenberg is a lover of color in all forms, only one of which is yarn. A frequent contributor to the Knit List, her knitting poems have been published in knitting guild newsletters nationwide and in *Interweave Knits'* subscriber newsletter.

Hannah Treworgy is a graduate of Mills College and currently lives in Jamaica Plain, Massachusetts. When she is not working (which is more often than she'd like these days), she keeps sane by singing in a women's a capella group, The Copley Cats. She hopes one day to knit as well as her sister.

Barbara Wagner is sixteen and rows for her school in Boston. She loves knitting socks to keep her feet warm when she's busy sitting in the sleet. In her spare time, she posts her art and writing on the Internet; see www.elfwood.lysator.liu.se/loth/c/e/cebbie/cebbie.html.

Beth Walker lives in Boulder, Colorado, with her family, too many dogs, and too many knitting projects. A reforming technical writer, she now pursues more interesting and less lucrative nonfiction and fiction. Hats off to 4-H and her mother for her early start as a knitter.

Molly Wolf, who usually writes God-stuff (three books published, two in the works), lives in Kingston, Ontario, with her husband, two almost grown sons, and two cats. Editing *KnitLit* has converted her to a fervent (if still inexpert) knitter with a growing stash problem. See www.sabbath-blessings.org.

Marge Wooley was raised in New Jersey but became an unofficial New Englander when she attended summer camp in Hillsboro, New Hampshire. After living in Colorado for twenty-six years she moved back to New Hampshire in 1995. Golf, always a passion, now has to compete with her knitting.

Dear Reader

Just to let you know:

First, don't miss the KnitLit website, www.knitlit.com. It provides you with information about both KnitLit volumes, contributors, charity knitting, knit-ins, and all sorts of links to other fascinating sites. You can even join our distribution mailing list!

Second, watch out for KnitLit the Third: We Spin More Yarns. Yes, we are planning a third volume. We'll be posting contributors' guidelines on the website, or you can reach us by e-mail at info@knitlit.com or at:

KnitLit
P.O. Box 3561
Amherst, MA 01004

We look forward to hearing from you.
Linda and Molly

Don't miss Linda Roghaar and Molly Wolf's first collection of stories, essays, anecdotes, and recollections celebrating the joys of knitting.

Knit Lit

Sweaters and Their Stories . . . and Other Writing About Knitting

0-609-80824-9
$13.00 paperback
(Canada: $20.00)